MICROWAVE
THE COOKING REVOLUTION

Jenny M. Webb

FORBES PUBLICATIONS

fp

641.7
SCHULTZ

© Forbes Publications Limited
Hartree House, Queensway,
London W2 4SH

All rights reserved
First published 1977 ISBN 0 901762 26 1
Reprinted March 1978

Printed in Great Britain by
Chapel River Press, Andover, Hants.

Contents

iii

List of figures, tables and photographs

Preface

The purpose of writing this book is to give a greater insight and knowledge to those who wish to obtain a fundamental appreciation of the concept of microwave ovens. It is hoped that it will create a greater understanding of an apparently simple appliance which, when used to its fullest extent, will enable the user to enjoy not only the everyday benefits in food preparation but to find a greater joy in creative cooking which so often is lacking due to the fast pace of life today.

It would be difficult to mention by name the many people who have given me both help and advice without which I could not have completed the various chapters of this book. However, I hope that they will forgive me for making a special mention of two of their number: Mr. Harry Barber, Senior Lecturer of Loughborough University of Technology and Secretary to the European Chapter of the International Microwave Power Institute, and Mr. Richard Harvey, OBE, Director of the Electricity Council's Appliance Testing Laboratories, as without their help and encouragement it would not have been possible for me to write *Microwave—the Cooking Revolution.*

J. M. W.

Introduction

In years to come the 20th century is likely to be regarded as one which was the beginning of the great technological advance. Certainly, during the lifetime of people living today we have been fortunate enough to see and experience many remarkable achievements. Nevertheless, to some, their children, life without a radio or television is something they can only think of in terms of history. This is indicative of the speed of change moving from extreme poverty and all it brings to that of a wealth which embraces health, comfort, education, leisure and convenience. The technological achievements in almost every area which one would care to examine are endless, but regardless of these it is still necessary for the human to sustain his body with food and it is generally accepted that the food will undergo some type of cooking operation before it is consumed.

Many foods eaten in the early 1900's are still eaten today, but the word 'variety' has entered onto the scene and as a result foods from the entire world beset many a table. Variety has been extended due to many reasons: more people travel abroad thus introducing the desire for different foods; the preservation and method of transportation of fresh produce has been improved; education has made people more aware of the nutritive values of food; farming methods have been streamlined; the standard of living is higher; and even two world wars have contributed and influenced the eating habits and life style of everyone.

The list could be endless, but even with all of these, foods in general are still cooked by applying heat and using some very well tried, even ancient methods.

The appliances used to achieve the desired result may have changed, but in principle the method of applying the energy to cook the food has hardly changed at all. However, the introduction of microwave ovens brings about a new concept of cooking food which will not necessarily cover every cooking method, but will certainly introduce a new thought pattern to the preparation and cooking of food today and in the years to come.

On the domestic front, in the UK, the microwave oven is relatively new, but it has been used extensively in the commercial environment for a good many years. Consequently it can be found not only in restaurants, pubs, clubs, hotels and canteens, but in such places as hospitals and even on planes and trains. Thus, it has already proved itself to be a useful piece of equipment able to supply and meet the demands and needs of many thousands of people.

Many think that the microwave oven is a development of the 1970's but it was first conceived when research was being carried out on radar during the second world war. However, it was not until the late 1940's that the first oven was produced in the United States of America, and later still, in 1955, that the first domestic microwave oven was introduced.

The word 'microwave' originated in 1940 and is defined in the Oxford English Dictionary as 'an electro-magnetic wave having a wave length of less than 20 cm', thus in using the term microwave oven the original meaning of the word has been retained. Since 1940 the whole concept of microwave cooking has moved forward in leaps and bounds and as a result the microwave oven is an ideal appliance for today's world, being versatile, economical, fast and easy to use.

It is versatile because so many operations such as thawing, heating, boiling, baking, roasting, poaching and even softening and melting may be carried out using the same piece of equipment. It is economical for the simple reason that as the energy produced is being directed into the food, it is not being wasted elsewhere, and as a result, the overall fuel consumption is reduced as is the time spent working in the kitchen. It is fast because thawed, heated, or cooked food can be produced in a fraction of the time that it would normally take when using conventional methods. It is easy to use as in general there are only two controls and learning how to operate them is simple and straightforward.

There are many other advantages, such as being able to cook food in the container in which it is going to be served; the kitchen will remain cooler as there is no oven preheating needed; and as it cooks so quickly there is very little heat loss through the oven walls. Because the speed of the cooking is so fast, and the cooking operation is carried out in the confined area of the oven, smells are reduced and they therefore do not have time to permeate the atmosphere. The oven interior does not get too hot thus it is not possible for foods to 'burn on', and the result is that oven cleaning is almost a thing of the past. The hazard of handling hot dishes is virtually non existent—it is the food which gets hot, not the containers and oven, and last but not least, by virtue of the design of the microwave oven and its method of heating and cooking, decorating the kitchen becomes a less frequent chore. It would therefore seem that with so many advantages the use of the conventional cooker and other appliances would be totally unnecessary. But this is not the case as the microwave oven has its limitations like many other appliances. Nevertheless, the microwave oven and conventional appliances can complement each other and as a result make life easier for all those who are involved in the preparation and cooking of food.

CHAPTER 1

How a microwave oven works
Security in design
How a microwave oven cooks food
Siting the microwave oven

How a microwave oven works

Many people have little idea as to how they are able to enjoy the pleasure of a television or a radio but the mere mention of a microwave oven always seems to create interest. The reason for this is difficult to ascertain, but perhaps it is because in comparison to the conventional methods of cooking it resembles something of a magician's box producing thawed, heated and cooked food with no apparent heat. Thus, like most magic tricks the average person has an inbuilt curiosity to know how and why.

Usually most people think in terms of electrical energy being transmitted through a wire. Electro-magnetic waves can, however, transmit energy through space. The waves, with the exception of visible light, cannot be seen but the benefits of X-rays, infra-red radiation, and even the pleasure of television and radio all result from the transmission of energy by electro-magnetic waves. Heating food in a microwave oven, too, is the result of using electro-magnetic waves. All these phenomena are due to electro-magnetic waves within defined frequency bands in the electro-magnetic spectrum. As can be seen in Figure 1 the spectrum is very long and the microwaves only cover a very small part of it.

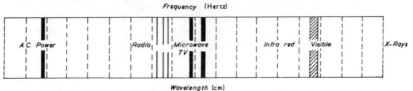

Figure 1. **The electro-magnetic spectrum**

1

A basic microwave oven

As with all appliances the microwave oven can and does have various features which will change the appearance of the basic unit. Nevertheless, the principle of producing microwaves remains the same. See Figure 2.

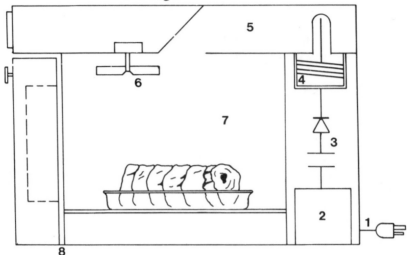

Figure 2. **A basic microwave oven**

1. The flexible cord—The appliance is switched on and the electricity flows to the
2. Power transformer—which increases the 240 alternating voltage to a very high alternating voltage. This passes into
3. A high voltage rectifier and capacitor—which changes the high alternating voltage into unidirectional, i.e. direct voltage. The unidirectional voltage is applied to
4. The magnetron—which converts this direct voltage to a very high frequency alternating voltage and so generates microwave energy.
This energy is then conducted via
5. The waveguide—which directs it towards the oven cavity.
As the microwaves enter the oven
6. The wave stirrer (paddle)—turns very slowly to distribute the microwaves evenly around the oven.
7. The oven cavity—being constructed of metal safely contains the microwaves which are deflected off the walls and base to be absorbed by the food.
8. The oven door—and the surrounding frame is provided with special seals constructed to ensure that the microwaves are confined within the cavity. In addition it is so arranged that as the door is opened the microwave power is automatically shut off.

Security in Design

All reputable microwave oven manufacturers will fully ensure that their appliance is electrically safe and that the radiation

2

leakage is insignificant. However, as with all electrical appliances, a further guarantee of safety is the Approval BEAB label for household appliances, or the Electricity Council label for commercial catering equipment. These labels confirm that the appliance meets safety requirements and operates within the microwave leakage limits set out in the appropriate British Standard Specification. These are for domestic ovens, BS 3456: Specification for Household Electrical Appliances: Part 2: Section 2.33: 1976 'Microwave Ovens'; and for the commercial catering microwave ovens, BS 5175: 1976 'The Specification for the Safety of Commercial Electrical Appliances Using Microwave Energy for Heating Foodstuffs'.

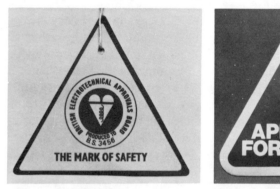

Figure 3. **BEAB label**   Figure 4. **Electricity Council label**

The requirements of these two Standards are basically the same, and are very stringent as is the case with all electrical safety Standards, but in the case of the microwave ovens they also take into account not only the limits on the leakage of microwave energy but also the maintenance of these limits throughout the life of the appliance. An example of this is the oven door which must have at least two interlocks, so that if one fails it is impossible to operate the oven with the door open. The radiation leakage measured at a distance of 50 mm (2 in.) from the door must not exceed at any time during the life of the microwave oven 5 mW/cm². Indeed, leakage from a typical oven in a new condition is only about 0·03 mW/cm².

It must be remembered that the radiation spreads out when it escapes through any leakage point so that the amount of radiation

3

falling on any surface decreases very rapidly as the distance from the source increases; thus, for example, if the maximum measured leakage was 5 mW/cm² at the oven door it would have decreased to 0·002 mW/cm² if measured at the distance of an arm's length.

The word radiation is one which is used very freely and is often misused. Radiation falls into two categories, particle radiation and electro-magnetic radiation. There is no particle radiation from a microwave oven. Electro-magnetic radiation can itself be further sub-divided into ionizing and non-ionizing radiation, the energy effect being greatest at very high frequencies (above ultra violet). When organisms are exposed to high frequency ionizing rays a chemical change takes place in the cellular structure, but with non-ionizing rays there is no chemical change in organisms. Furthermore, ionizing rays have an accumulative effect whereas non-ionizing rays have to the best of current knowledge a non-accumulative effect, but as non-ionizing rays can cause a change in temperature the benefits of cooking and heating in a microwave oven can be enjoyed by all. To put the subject into perspective and to refer to terms which may be more commonly used, it can be said that in general ionizing rays are those such as gamma-rays, x-rays and ultra-violet rays. Non-ionizing rays are those such as light waves and radio waves and microwaves. To quote Professor James Van Allen, of the University of Iowa, who was the discoverer of the radiation belts around the earth—'My judgement of microwave oven hazard is about the same as the likelihood of getting a skin tan from moonlight.'

How a microwave oven is able to cook food

Microwave ovens can be used almost anywhere by anyone having little or no knowledge of cooking. However, the more skill a user has in the art of food preparation the quicker and greater use can be made of the oven.

Three terms generally employed when discussing the conventional process of cooking food are: conduction, convection and radiation. Depending upon the type of cooking operation being carried out one or more of these methods could be used. Briefly, conduction is when heat is transferred from a hot to a cold surface which is in contact with it, e.g. frying a cold egg on a

4

hot griddle. Convection is when heat is transferred from one place to another by movement of the hot material e.g. baking a cake in a hot oven where heat is transferred through movement of the hot air. Radiation is when the heat travels through space and is converted back into heat when absorbed e.g. cooking a piece of steak under a hot grill.

Microwaves are essentially of this third type but they are different from the conventional type of cooking radiation in that they can penetrate more deeply into the food being cooked before they are absorbed and turned into heat. However, microwaves act differently with different substances, they are either *reflected, transmitted* or *absorbed.*

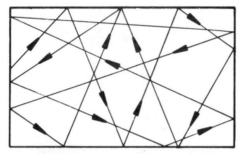

Figure 5. **The reflection of microwaves in an oven**

Metal *reflects* microwaves thus the oven interiors are constructed with metal to reflect the waves towards the food, and this is also the reason why metal containers are not suitable receptacles for use in the oven as the food would be deprived of the waves and as a result no cooking would be achieved.

Figure 6. **Microwaves being transmitted through a container**

5

Microwaves are *transmitted* through many materials, such as glass, china and some plastics; they pass through them almost as if they were not there. As a result most of these materials may be used as containers to accommodate food, but see Chapter 7 *Cooking Containers and Utensils.*

Food and liquid, because of their structure, *absorb* microwaves and by doing so enable food to be heated and cooked.

Figure 7. **Food absorbing microwaves**

What happens to the food as the microwaves are absorbed? Food is made up of millions of molecules and each of these react to the microwaves in a way similar to that of a compass reacting to a magnet. Place a compass on a table and then put a magnet next to it, immediately the needle will swing round to point to the magnet. Move the magnet to the opposite side and at once the needle will turn to point in that direction.

So it is with the microwaves and the food molecules, as the waves are absorbed by the food each molecule is excited and moves back and forth at a speed of well over two thousand million times a second. In this way heat is generated and the food is heated and cooked in a very short time.

Siting the microwave oven

Although cooking in the microwave oven is fast the wattage of the appliance is not particularly high, which means in general that fixed wiring is not required. Thus, once a suitable plug has been fitted it becomes an appliance that can be used almost anywhere. In addition to which, it is not an appliance that takes up very much space and being relatively light in weight may be transported from room to room without too many difficulties.

The Moffat microwave oven model 4000

The natural siting for a microwave oven would be the kitchen and it may be accommodated on any firm table or work surface at any desired level. However, providing a suitable air space is left around the oven, there is no reason why it should not be built into a kitchen unit and become part of the kitchen design. Nevertheless, because of its convenient size, it could be accommodated in a breakfast or dining room, as it is here that food can be heated or cooked and served directly to the table. This may be of particular benefit to those having families eating at irregular times, as even the young children could quickly and safely re-heat a meal or cook breakfast for themselves. Although it is not suggested that the microwave oven be permanently accommodated in a bedroom it is certainly a useful place to put it if there is sickness in the house as nursing a sick patient is a tiring enough business for both the patient and 'nurse' without the extra carrying that food preparation in the kitchen entails. By siting the microwave oven in the bedroom the patient can enjoy hot drinks and food at any time of day or night without the necessity of inconveniencing anyone else. For those who live in bedsits, where

7

cooking facilities are limited or difficult, the microwave oven could certainly be of benefit especially as it can be readily moved as part of the furniture.

A further consideration is that of entertaining and even though the weather in the United Kingdom is not generally conducive to outside eating the microwave oven could be utilised indoors to add to the entertainment scene, being both quick and convenient and fun to use. The fact that it is called a microwave 'oven' suggests to some that it is a kitchen appliance, but it is obvious that it will lend itself to almost any situation and as a result could prove to be the most well used, popular piece of equipment in any house.

Many brush off the art of cooking as something anyone can do, indeed, most people tend to produce and cook complete meals with such apparent effortless ease that this adds to the misconception. Basic food preparation is not simple in itself, but to be able to calculate cooking operations for several types of foods and to plate them all at the same time would send many rushing for a computer. Cooking is rather more complicated than imagined at first glance as it is very difficult to produce a full meal in a very short time for obvious reasons. So what does the brain of the cook have to calculate when preparing any foods to be cooked by conventional methods. What is the menu? How is it to be prepared? What type of cooking is needed? Is it to be by conduction, radiation or convection or all three? Would the oven or grill have to be preheated? Does boiling water have to be obtained? What temperatures are to be used? How long has each food to be cooked? At what time should the cooking operation be started to ensure that all of it will be ready together? It is at this point that the benefits of a microwave oven can be appreciated, as it does not detract from the art of cooking, but will allow the user to produce foods both quickly and efficiently without too many complicated calculations masking the final effort.

To use the microwave oven is very simple and it is not absolutely necessary to be aware of all the factors which can affect the heating and cooking results. Generally, it is just a case of following the microwave oven manufacturers' cookery book and excellent results can be obtained every time. Nevertheless, just as with conventional cooking, certain factors can affect the results

8

and although these, in many instances, are the same, it is interesting to study them in more depth.

In general, when cooking by conventional methods, the cooking temperatures have to be selected with care. Should the temperature (heat) be too high the outside of the food would cook or possibly burn before the heat had had sufficient time to reach the centre of it. Consequently, the food would give the appearance of being cooked but on cutting, the interior would be 'raw'. However, the microwave oven simplifies the art. Therefore, the selection of cooking temperatures and the conventional methods of applying heat may be disregarded as it is simply a question of thinking of time in relation to the quantity of food being prepared.

Although the heating and cooking times relate directly to the food, it is a fact that the structure and condition of the food itself is very important, and that foods and liquids vary in the amount of heat required to raise their temperature. Thus such things as the moisture content, the size, the shape, the initial food temperature, and the amount of food can make a difference to the cooking time. Indeed, *the container* in which it is being cooked can also have an influence. So far as the container is concerned, the simple rules to observe are (a) choose a shape which will fit the shape of the food; (b) when heating or cooking liquid foods ensure that it is of such a depth that the food will not boil over; and (c) be sure to use a container which is suitable for use in the microwave oven. See Chapter 7 *Cooking Utensils and Containers.*

CHAPTER 2

The art of thawing, heating and cooking food in a microwave oven

Handling processes of foods and containers, standing time, thawing foods, covering and wrapping food, looking at individual foods

As in conventional cooking the *initial temperature of the food* will make a difference to the heating or cooking time. An example of this: on a hot summer's day the cold water drawn from the tap is much warmer than it would be during a cold winter's day, thus, the same quantity of water boiled in the summer will take a shorter time than the same quantity of water boiled in the winter. Cooking in a microwave oven is exactly the same, the colder the food placed in the microwave oven the longer it will take to cook. However, it is important to note that the times being discussed are not minutes and hours but seconds and minutes.

The *thickness and shape of the food* is also important; some examples: a long thin piece of food will take a shorter time to cook than a short fat piece, even though it may be of the same type and weight. The shape of a fish is such that the body is thick whereas the tail is thin and almost transparent, thus the tail would be dehydrated before the body was cooked. In this instance, the tail would be protected, possibly by a small piece of foil to reflect the microwaves from this area and the heat from the body would be sufficient to cook the tail. A plated meal comprising meat, potatoes and carrots would not only be different in shape but also in height. Therefore, to overcome the inconvenience of one food heating more quickly than the other a uniform arrangement of the height would be likely to suffice.

The *volume of the food* will influence the cooking time and the greater the volume the longer it will take to cook, but this is not on a proportional basis; a simple product such as a small jacket potato will take about $3\frac{1}{2}$–4 minutes, two potatoes about $6\frac{1}{2}$–7

10

minutes, 3 potatoes 8½–9 minutes.

The *density of the food* will vary and those foods which are light and porous such as bread or pastry will absorb the microwaves much more quickly than a product such as meat which is dense and heavy. Thus, the light and porous food will cook more quickly.

The *moisture content of the food* also has a bearing; the more moisture or water in food the more energy is required to heat it.

Handling processes of foods and containers

The greatest penetration of microwaves is at the first 35–50 mm (1½–2 in.) of the food and this decreases as the microwaves pass through the subsequent food layers. Nevertheless, due to the molecule agitation and the heat generated there is sufficient heat available in the food itself to continue the cooking of the food mass by conduction. Thus, it is possible to thaw, heat or cook almost anything, from a small thin piece of bacon to a family size joint of meat. However, as the moisture content in the food will vary it could so happen that small spots or areas of the food could cook more quickly than other parts and as a result 'hot spots' would occur. This is because microwaves heat water more quickly and consequently give up most of their energy to the moister parts of the food. The simple method to avoid this inconvenience is to turn or *rotate* the container which is holding the food around during the cooking operation giving a 90 or 180 degree turn. The frequency of this depends upon what type and quantity of food is

Figure 8. **Illustration showing dish rotation**

11

being cooked but when thawing, heating or cooking small quantities dish rotation is not usually necessary as all the microwaves are concentrating on the one food item.

In the case of liquids or such liquid items as casseroles rather than rotate the dish it is better to occasionally *stir* the contents to ensure an even heating result.

For large solid foods such as joints of meat or poultry both dish rotation or stirring are not suitable therefore these foods should generally be *turned over* to obtain the maximum benefit of the microwaves.

Standing time

Because of the unique method of using the microwaves to heat and cook food, a standing time should be given at the completion of the operation. This time is usually the time it takes to transport the food from the kitchen to the dining room but in the instance of larger foods such as meat it can be anything up to 20 minutes. The reason for having a standing time is simply because even when the microwave energy has been switched off the food continues to cook by conduction. Thus, this time allows and ensures that the heat within the food is uniform, and as in the case of large items like meat that the very centre is cooked. Recipe books take this into account and will usually state should a standing time be required. Standing time may also be referred to as the 'carry over' cooking. However, where a conventional recipe is used for the first time it is advisable to cook for about a quarter of the conventional time and to give a standing time based on a similar food product in the manufacturer's book. It is also important to remember that any food which is overcooked will dehydrate and there is no return; however, should it be undercooked a minute or two back in the oven will invariably give perfection with little if any effort.

Thawing food

Thawing food is a simple operation and is controlled either manually or in some ovens by an automatic device fitted to the oven. The method employed is by 'pulsing' the microwaves, and the total time given would be dependent upon the quantity and the food being thawed. However, the principle is to have the oven switched on for a specified period of time then to switch it off for a short period. This sequence would be continued until the food has thawed. Sometimes, this procedure may be described as subjecting the food to 'short bursts of microwaves'.

The simple explanation for using the microwave oven in this manner is quite logical. When food is frozen, ice crystals form and these are not uniform in size. Some will be larger than others. Microwaves pass through ice almost as if it was transparent but the smaller crystals will melt first and because water has a higher absorption rate of energy than ice, these areas could then be at the cooking stage whilst other parts would still be in the icy state. The result—an unevenly thawed food item. However, by depriving the frozen food of energy by interrupting the microwaves, the still frozen areas have the opportunity to benefit from the conduction of heat accumulated in the lesser or unfrozen areas. The period during which no microwave energy is being used is sometimes described as the equalizing or rest period.

Amana model RR-4D with automatic defrost

An exclusive feature of one manufacturer is a mat and cover which is designed to reduce the likelihood of dehydration around the edges of frozen products during the thawing process.

The accessory comprises a round ceramic mat complete with a

13

metal cover, similar to that of a plate cover. As the cover has a plastics handle, and the underside also accommodates a ceramic disc enclosed in plastics, the microwaves are only able to pass through these areas. The ceramic is of a type which retains heat and therefore contributes to the thawing process.

To use the accessory the frozen food is placed in its container on the ceramic mat, covered with the metal cover and the oven is then operated in the usual manner.

Covering and wrapping foods

The first principle to apply is that of always following the instructions given in a microwave recipe book. Nevertheless, not every recipe or food item may be included in the book and it is at this stage that the following guidance may be useful.

Where foods need to be kept moist then the use of a cover or wrapping is used. A cover may be in the form of china, glass or cling type film but must not be metallic. See Chapter 7 *Utensils and Containers.*

Foods which are intended to be 'dry' such as breads, pastries and cakes should not in general be covered during cooking as this would make them 'soggy'. However, should these products be heated, then a piece of absorbent paper placed under the food will ensure that any moisture is not absorbed by the base of the food.

Some foods do not require a cover or wrapping but may be of the type which could splatter. In which case a piece of greaseproof paper or absorbent paper lightly placed over the food will be a simple method of allieviating the inconvenience.

A caution: covers and wrappings should always be fitted loosely or pierced to allow for some escape of steam. However, should this not be observed, there could be a possibility of hot steam being suddenly emitted as the cover or wrapping was removed. Therefore it is advisable to exercise care when carrying out this operation.

Looking at the individual foods

The versatility of a microwave oven is remarkable, covering a vast area of food preparation, and the following information will give some indication as to the basic principles for thawing, heating and cooking various foods. However, although the output of many ovens will be the same, should they not be then the times given could either be increased or decreased accordingly. Therefore, it should be noted that the times and methods given are only intended as a guide, and reference to the individual microwave oven manufacturer's instruction and recipe book should always be made.

Bread Many types of bread can be baked in the microwave oven, but they will not be browned or have a crisp crust. Nevertheless, if a soft crust is acceptable or a brown flour is being used, the microwave oven will produce a very palatable bread. Should a brown crust be required the microwave oven may be employed in conjunction with a conventional oven to speed up the cooking process. The bread being initially cooked in the microwave oven and then transferred to a very hot preheated conventional oven, and as a result the cooking would be finished and a brown crust would be obtained. In this instance, if for example a 500 gram (1 lb.) quantity was being baked the cooking time in the microwave oven would be about 3 minutes and the final cooking time in the conventional oven about 8 minutes.

The non-metallic container used for bread making should be greased, or lined with greaseproof paper or cling film and the operation carried out uncovered. It is not advisable to flour the container as this will create a cooked flour film on the final product.

Frozen breads can be thawed very quickly. A bread roll only takes about 15–20 seconds, but if more than one roll or piece of bread is being thawed, then the time would be increased. For example: one slice would take about 15 seconds, two slices 25 seconds, three slices 35 seconds. Bread rolls take a slightly shorter period and with most thawing operations it is advisable to rest the product for a minute or two before serving. During the thawing period the bread should be placed on a piece of absorbent paper or towel and should not be covered.

Frozen bread dough can be thawed and proved in a microwave oven and to complete the operation would take about 1 hour for a 500 gram (1 lb.) loaf. In this instance, the method used is that of subjecting the dough to bursts of microwave energy of approximately 3 minutes and then a 3 minute rest period. This operation would be continued until the dough had doubled in size but it could take twelve or more operations. Needless to say, it is still quicker than thawing at room temperature.

A microwave oven is not able to toast bread, but if bread is toasted in the conventional manner then this can be used as a base for toppings which may be heated or cooked afterwards in the microwave oven. For example: melted cheese on toast would take about 15–20 seconds. The oven is also capable of dehydrating bread and therefore if rusks are required they can be obtained in a very few minutes; however, if reheating bread which has been left for too long, dehydration, in this instance, would result in a tough rubbery product. Thus, whether bread is being cooked or reheated it is advisable to undercook or heat and to be aware that the centre of the product will invariably be hotter than the outside.

Beverages Apart from the everyday beverages, the microwave oven seems to give extra spice to hot drinks such as mulled cider, wine and hot toddies and even children seem to enjoy their milk shakes served hot. Other advantages can be enjoyed; drinks may be heated in the drinking container as and when required, and should a drink be left to get cold it need not be thrown away but quickly and simply reheated.

Thawing frozen drinks is an easy operation, and this even applies to tinned drinks which must be removed from the tin before heating by putting it in hot water for a minute or two and then placing the contents in a suitable uncovered non-metallic container.The thawing time would be about 2 minutes but to speed up the operation the liquid should be broken up with a fork and stirred occasionally. A simple way to remove the frozen contents from a tin is to open both ends and then push the solid block from one end.

Any non-metallic drinking container used uncovered is suitable for use. However, should the handle be glued on it is not recommended for use. If milk is being heated it does have a tendency to rise up in the container, therefore it is advisable to make sure that the cup, etc. will allow for this. The sugar and the coffee or chocolate powder can be added to the cold liquid before heating but this sometimes causes the drink to 'froth' during the heating period in which case the sugar and powder may be added

16

after the milk has been heated.

The time taken to heat any liquid will depend upon its initial temperature and the size of cup or mug selected. As a guide, 1 cup of water would take $1-1\frac{1}{2}$ minutes, 2 cups $2-2\frac{1}{2}$ minutes, 3 cups $3\frac{1}{4}-4$ minutes. Nevertheless, on some occasions it may be quicker and more convenient to use an electric kettle if more than 500ml (1 pint) of water is to be heated.

Bottling Fruit bottling may be carried out in some microwave ovens but it is very important as with conventional bottling methods that the microwave oven manufacturers instructions are followed. However, if it is recommended, small jars are generally the best to use and the syrup is made in the microwave oven, after which the prepared fruit is added and then cooked in the jar. In addition it must be remembered that because the syrup is hot the jars would become hot and careful handling of the jars is essential, and that unless specifically stated by the microwave oven manufacturer, metal tops must not be employed.

Biscuits Some conventional biscuit recipes tend to spread in the microwave oven when they are being cooked. But biscuit mixtures which are to be cut after cooking appear to be more successful than the individual ones. Manufacturers do give some recipes but it is worth experimenting although it should be remembered that golden browning cannot be achieved. However, experiments can be made when cooking the biscuits in the conventional manner. A few uncooked biscuits could be put aside and then cooked in the microwave oven. In general a container and covering is not required and a sheet of greaseproof paper or a flat greased non-metallic plate should suffice but, as in cake making, flour should not be used as this would create a flour crust on the cooked product.

To thaw frozen biscuits they should be stood on an absorbent piece of paper or towel and the time taken to thaw will be minimal. One biscuit could take about 15 seconds but this time would have to be increased according to the number being defrosted.

Confectionery The making of sweets comes back into its own and by using the microwave oven it seems to be easier, not so involved, and the risk of scorching is lessened, especially where high temperatures are required. As in conventional sweet making the non-metallic container must be at least two or three times larger than the quantity being made and should not be covered. Care must be exercised when handling the container as the heat from the melted sugar will be absorbed by the container itself and consequently can make it hot. If a sugar thermometer is being used it must not at any time be left in the oven but any temperature measurements made outside the oven. Microwave oven manufacturers' recipe books, especially those from the USA, usually give a special section on the subject of confectionery and the range is extensive covering both high and low temperature sweet making.

Cake making The subject of cake making is vast, especially in the United Kingdom, as cakes tend to be something everyone seems to enjoy eating at any time of the day, and often the recipes have been handed down from mother to daughter.

A microwave oven is able to thaw almost any frozen cake with only a few exceptions and even in these instances a user may succeed. One of the exceptions is where a cake has been filled or decorated with fresh cream, or butter cream, in which case it is likely that the cream would thaw more rapidly than the cake itself. Therefore, it is wiser not to thaw in the oven. However, if it is essential that the cake be thawed quickly then it is better to subject the cake to the microwaves for a very short time to speed up the total thawing process, and then to leave the cake to stand and finish thawing at normal room temperature. As with most microwave operations it is essential not to overheat the product, but for a 20cm (8in.) cake it is only necessary to subject it to about 3 minutes of microwave energy and then leave it to stand for 5 minutes before serving. If the cake is not quite thawed a minute or two back in the oven will quickly achieve the desired result. Where small cakes, such as fairy cakes are being thawed, then the time allowed is very much less. For example, one cake would take about 30 seconds and then should be left to stand for 2 minutes. If a number of small cakes are in the oven being thawed the time is increased, but as soon as any one small cake feels warm to the touch then it should be removed immediately.

Cooking cakes in a microwave oven is possible, but in general some modifications would have to be made to the recipe.

Any non-metallic container may be used and this would include paper and even ice cream cones. If a solid container is employed then it may be greased or lined with greaseproof paper or cling type film. However, it is not advisable to use a floured container as this would result in a crust forming on the cooked product. A round uncovered non-metallic container is usually the best shape in which to cook a layer cake and for this size it is better to cook one at a time rather than trying to cook two together. In addition to which, as cakes rise very well in a microwave oven any container should not be filled by more than half its capacity of uncooked mixture.

As the cooking is such a speedy operation, it is possible that cakes may start to rise unevenly but should this occur it is simply a case of turning the container. In some instances, the container is given a quarter turn about every $1\frac{1}{2}$–2 minutes and the total cooking time would be in the region of 6 minutes. As would be expected, small cakes, such as fairy cakes take a very much shorter cooking time. For example one would take 15–20 seconds, two 30–40 seconds, six $1\frac{1}{2}$–2 minutes, and twelve 3–4 minutes. The method of checking as to whether or not a cake is cooked is by the conventional method of inserting a cocktail stick or skewer when the cake is removed from the oven—if the stick or skewer is clean, the cake is cooked.

As with most microwave oven operations, especially where certain products are being cooked for the first time, it is better to underbake rather than overbake, and once the cake is removed from the oven it should be left in the container for about 10 minutes before removing.

It is possible to use conventional recipes, but these may need adjustment as sometimes the taste of the raising agent is more noticeable. Should this be the case then it is worth trying reducing the raising agent by up to 25%. Slack mixtures of the batter consistency, seem to be the most successful, and many of the existing cake mixes available on the market can be successfully used, but it must be remembered that the dark golden brown colour achieved in the conventional oven cannot be obtained in the microwave oven.

Nevertheless, if the cake is coloured itself, e.g. chocolate or the cake is to be iced or decorated then the overall colour would be of less importance. On the whole cakes which contain a high proportion of dried fruit do not cook well in the microwave oven and in these instances it may be preferred to cook them in the conventional oven taking advantage of long slow cooking. At the moment there are very few cookery books available in the United Kingdom on the subject of cake baking, but with the growing popularity of microwave ovens, it is more than likely that these will be more readily available in the future. Meanwhile, for those who use a microwave oven, the microwave oven manufacturers' cookery books do include sections on cake making and many of these recipes can be readily made or adapted and enjoyed.

Eggs and cheese Both eggs and cheese are foods which require special care when being cooked in a microwave oven as these foods cook in such a very short time that seconds can make all the difference to the end result. Eggs and cheese can be easily over-cooked and as a result they can become tough and rubbery and most unacceptable. As with other foods cooked in the microwave oven, it is better to err on the side of undercooking and allow the heat within the food to gently finish the process. One operation which is definitely taboo is that of cooking eggs in their shells, the result is a disaster. The reason for this is that pressure builds up within the egg at a very fast rate adding stresses to the egg shell, which in the end causes the egg to 'explode'. This not only creates a cleaning problem never experienced before but the impact within the oven could cause such damage that a service call would prove to be very costly. In general, it is better to use eggs at room temperature rather than from the refrigerator, and if they are to be 'fried' or 'poached' the egg yolk should be pricked with a cocktail stick. By doing this, it will prevent a pressure build up under the membrane of the yolk and thus avoid the yolk bursting during cooking. In some instances the microwave oven manufacturer may suggest that the white should also be pricked, but it is wise to check the instruction book as each manufacturer will have his own tips when it comes to cooking eggs.

Scrambled eggs are a delight to cook as the texture achieved can be varied to suit every taste, ranging from a wet creamy mixture to a solid mass. To achieve this, it is simply a question of removing the mixture from the dish at the desired time. To scramble two eggs, the eggs, melted butter, and milk are lightly

20

beaten together and put in an uncovered non-metallic container, such as a soup dish. They are cooked for about 1 minute, the mixture is then stirred and returned to the oven for a minute or so. Any seasoning required is added before serving. If more eggs are to be scrambled and a deeper container used, then the times would increase accordingly.

Dishes made with cheese are always very tasty and popular and the microwave oven manufacturers' recipe books do include a range that will appeal to most. However, if a golden finish is required it will be necessary to put the made dish under a hot preheated grill to achieve the desired appearance.

Fondue is an interesting dish to serve and the microwave oven makes the preparation easy, as it is simply a question of placing the cheese and the appropriate additions into a covered dish to cook. To make a fondue of 500 grams (1 lb.) quantity would only take about seven minutes.

Fish For those who are lovers of fish, the cooked fish results from a microwave oven will delight them. And for those who are not usually fish lovers, it is likely that they will find a new meaning and pleasure in eating it. In addition to which a further consideration is that of odour, and as the fish has been cooked quickly there tends to be less smell permeating the house than would be usually found if the conventional cooking methods had been used.

There are many fish recipes available and most of these can be successfully and quickly made in the microwave oven. To cook fish from the raw state is both fast and simple; if, for example, a 500 gram (1 lb.) quantity is used it is simply a question of brushing the fish with melted unsalted butter, sprinkling with pepper to taste, placing into a shallow covered non-metallic container or wrapping in cling film and cooking for approximately 6 minutes. Fish which is rather thick should be turned over half way during the cooking period. As white fish will not be coloured it may be necessary to brown it quickly under a hot grill or to serve it with a sauce. However, fish such as kippers, smoked haddock and trout are likely to be considered acceptable due to their own distinctive colourings.

Thawing frozen fish presents no difficulties and fillets may be thawed in seconds. As fish thaws so very quickly it is usually

Garnishing a fish dish. *Apollo Enterprises*

better to partially thaw it and to give short bursts of microwave energy and short rest periods. In all 500 grams (1 lb.) of frozen fish takes something like 2 minutes. As this type of operation is so quick it is always advisable to cook the fish immediately it has been defrosted.

Fruit Both fresh and frozen fruit may be thawed, heated and cooked without losing their original shape and colour, and in many instances the addition of water is not necessary; this is especially the case where frozen fruits are being thawed as there will be a sufficient amount of water available in the melted ice.

For any operation a covered container should be used but it should not be so tightly covered that steam is unable to escape.

When thawing frozen fruit it is wise to check its condition fairly frequently and, to aid in the thawing, the fruit should be gently broken up with a fork during the operation. The thawing time is very fast taking only something like 2–3 minutes to thaw a 250 gram (8 oz.) quantity, but a better result is obtained if the fruit is partially thawed and then left to stand for a few minutes before serving.

The preparation for the cooking of fresh fruit is as would be normally employed; that of washing, peeling, coring, stoning, and slicing or chopping. If desired sugar or flavourings are sprinkled onto the fruit and the fruit should be stirred once during the operation. The cooking time for hard fruits will be about 8–10 minutes, and for softer fruits 3–5 minutes.

Whether thawing, heating or cooking the best policy is to undercook and allow the fruit to finish off using its own heat.

Should items having skins be cooked whole e.g. baked apples, the skins should be pricked, cut or pierced. This is done to prevent them bursting during the cooking process due to a build up of pressure under the skin. As the stirring of whole fruit may not be convenient the container should be given a 90° or 180° turn during the process to ensure that the fruit is being evenly cooked.

Frying It is accepted and a known fact that any frying operation carried out in the conventional manner whether it be deep fat or shallow fat frying should not be done without someone being in attendance and care is always necessary. In view of this, and because the microwave oven gives a unique method of heating and cooking it is not possible to employ the microwave oven to heat fat and oils for these types of operations, and this is discouraged by all microwave oven manufacturers. Nevertheless, it is possible to sauté vegetables and the like and even to 'fry an egg' but in these instances the instructions given in the manufacturer's book should always be adhered to.

Meat and poultry Thawing and cooking meat and poultry in the microwave oven is simple, but gives further pleasure in that it can be carried out so very quickly that as a result there is no need to sit around starving whilst waiting in hungry anticipation. In which case thawing and heating casseroles is of particular benefit, and reheating meals should they have become cold saves the chore of keeping food hot over a steaming pan of water. On the whole both fresh meat and poultry should always be defrosted before cooking to ensure the best results but the exception could occur where the quantity is very small, in which case, the thawing and cooking may be carried out almost simultaneously. As with all times quoted in this book, the following times must only be taken as approximate and the microwave oven manufacturer's recipe book should always be referred to.

Unlike conventional cooking procedures meat and poultry

should not be seasoned with salt as this absorbs the moisture which in turn toughens the outer layer of the food. If salt is required, then it is simply a question of adding it after the cooking operation has been completed. Meats which are normally reliant on long slow cooking to break down the fibres and make them tender, such as stewing steak, are not in general very suitable for the microwave oven, as the speed with which the oven operates is too fast to allow the meat time to tenderise. Thus, in these cases, it is usually better to braise or stew the meat in the conventional manner. Nevertheless, if a casserole has been frozen after cooking, or has been refrigerated, it can be quickly and successfully thawed and heated for a meal.

Both meat and poultry when roasted in the microwave oven

Turkey roast. *Litton Microwave Cooking Products Ltd*

can deceive the person who is used to the conventional methods of cooking, as it gives the appearance of being cooked on the exterior, when in fact the interior is undercooked. Although meat and poultry can be roasted in a non-metallic dish with just a covering to avoid undue splashing of the fats and juices, the use of

24

a roasting bag would probably be preferred as this not only contains the juices but tends to give an even and better colour to the product. In this case, it is just a question of placing the food in the bag securing the end with a piece of string, remembering that metal ties would not be suitable in the microwave oven, and making a small slit in the bag to allow the steam to escape. The food is then placed in a dish to cook for the appropriate cooking time. Half way through the cooking time the joint or poultry should be turned over and then the remaining time given. The whole operation is just as simple if not more so than cooking by conventional means.

However, at this point there would be a slight change. On removal from the oven, the meat or poultry is wrapped in foil with the shiny side down and left to stand for about 15–20 minutes which allows the heat within the joint or poultry to be conducted right through to the very centre, and on carving it will still prove to be both succulent and hot to eat, It is interesting to note that during the standing time the internal temperature of the meat will increase by some 5°–8°C (10°–15°F) and should a meat thermometer be inserted at this time the temperature rise can easily be observed. Therefore, a meat thermometer is a useful aid in this respect, especially for the new microwave oven user. However, it is essential that at no time must the thermometer be left in the microwave oven during the cooking process. Nevertheless, it is advisable to follow the microwave oven manufacturer's instructions, especially in the case of meat and poultry and it is better to undercook rather than to overcook to avoid the food dehydrating. As a basic microwave oven is not able to produce a crisp brown appearance on smaller cuts of meat or poultry then, should this be required, the food may be either quickly browned under a preheated grill or lightly fried in a pan. However, if a microwave oven browning plate is being employed this would not be necessary. In general the easiest joint to roast is one which has been boned and rolled, as this gives an even thickness of solid meat, but this does not rule out the cooking of meat or poultry on the bone which can be done most successfully.

As the method of cooking meat and poultry is slightly different to that used in conventional ovens so the actual cooking time per pound is also different, being very much shorter, as can be seen in Table 1.

Table 1			
Times given are per 500 grams (1 lb.)			
Meat	Rare Minutes	Medium Minutes	Well done Minutes
Beef boned	6–7	7–8½	8½–10
With bone	5½–6½	6½–7½	7½–9
Lamb (leg or shoulder)		7	8–8½
Pork (shoulder)			10–13
Veal (rolled)			10–11½
Poultry			6–8

One of the boons of the microwave oven is the speed at which it thaws food and this is a particular benefit in the case of meat and poultry. Apart from the obvious benefit of being able to thaw meat and poultry at a time which is convenient to the user, the speed of a microwave oven encourages the user to ensure that it is really thawed. In general meat takes about 2 minutes a pound to thaw, and poultry 2 to 3 minutes to the pound, and during this time should be turned over half way through the operation, after which it is removed from the microwave oven and left to rest (equalise) for about 15–20 minutes. Most microwave oven manufacturers will advise the user to carry out the operation in stages by subjecting the meat to bursts of microwave energy, i.e. two minutes on and two minutes off. So far as smaller cuts of meat are concerned, i.e. a piece of steak, the thawing time may be shortened as the need to use any conductivity is reduced due to the thickness of the meat being less. If the user wishes to retain the thawed meat juices, the joint can be placed on a saucer and this will act as a simple juice retaining dish.

Pastry The cooking of raw pastry in the microwave oven is not always successful and in some cases it is better to cook it by conventional methods. Nevertheless, the concept of pastry cooked in a microwave oven should not be abandoned. Short crust pastry and strudel pastry are relatively successfully cooked as open flan cases or a strudel dish. Where double crusts are needed, such as with fruit pies, the result is unacceptable as the

26

filling tends to cook and bubble over before the pastry has been cooked. In certain instances it is possible to cook small pieces of puff pastry and the like by turning it over during the cooking period and this can be light and flaky as a result. However, in this instance it is worth carrying out some experiments to establish whether or not it is acceptable and to be aware that the pastry will not be browned.

To cook a shortcrust 150 mm (6 in.) pastry flan will take about 4 minutes, but the method of preparing the container is a matter of choice. An uncovered non-metallic plate pie dish is an acceptable shape and this may be lined with the pastry which has been well pricked to avoid it bubbling. However, rather than prick the shell a better result may be achieved by lining the container with the pastry, then placing a piece of absorbent paper over it, and on top of this putting a slightly smaller plate pie dish. This will then contribute to the pastry case holding its shape during the initial cooking time. After about $2\frac{1}{2}$ minutes both the retaining dish and paper should be carefully removed and then the flan in its original container returned to the oven to cook for a further minute or two. As with any flan case it can be used to accommodate fillings and in these instances the microwave oven may be used to cook them most successfully. Biscuit crust flans are very satisfactory and simple to make in the microwave oven; this may be done by melting the butter in the oven, adding the crushed biscuits and pressing into shape in the flan dish. In the space of a minute or two it can be cooked in the microwave oven.

Home cooked tarts, etc., can be cooked and frozen in advance and then quickly thawed in the microwave oven. In this instance the products should be placed on absorbent paper, and given short bursts of microwave energy.

The microwave oven is a perfect way in which to reheat home made or shop bought pies or tarts as the contents get piping hot in minutes. In addition to which individual portions are easily reheated if there is someone about who does not enjoy cold tarts or pies.

Pasta, Rice, Cereals There are many recipes which use pasta, rice or cereals as a base and to discuss each as an individual dish would be difficult. Thus, this section only takes into consideration the basic cooking methods and it should be noted that it is not intended to imply that other dishes may not be prepared and cooked. Most microwave oven manufacturers' recipe books will include a section on the subject of pasta, rice and cereal dishes and this will cover any specific requirements.

Pasta may be cooked in the microwave oven but the time taken is frequently on a par with the time taken by using the conventional methods. However, whichever method is selected by a user the microwave oven may be usefully employed to reheat the spaghetti, macaroni, or noodles.

It is difficult to be explicit with regard to the cooking times as there are so many forms of pasta available, from the traditional to the fast or quick cooking types. Thus, the best instructions to follow are those given by the microwave oven manufacturer. Nevertheless, a broad rule of thumb with regard to quantities would be: to every two cups of pasta use six cups of water.

The non-metallic container employed to accommodate the pasta should be of a similar size to that used for conventional cooking, being large enough to contain the contents without 'boiling over' occurring. However, as to whether or not the container should be covered would be dependent upon the individual oven manufacturer's recommendation. But should a cover be used, then it is important not to fit it so tightly that steam is unable to escape.

The pasta should be put into boiling water and the water may be either boiled in a kettle or in the container in the oven. After which, salt, a drop of oil, and the pasta is added and given the appropriate cooking time. To achieve the required degree of cooking, the container should be covered and left to stand for at least ten minutes after cooking. After the standing period the pasta can be drained and rinsed as usual and if required reheated in the microwave oven.

To reheat pasta whether or not it has been refrigerated is a simple operation of placing it in a lightly covered container and heating it until it is steaming. During the reheating period it is advisable to stir the pasta at least once to ensure that it is evenly heated.

Rice, like pasta, may be cooked by either the conventional cooking method or in the microwave oven but again the oven is

28

very useful for reheating purposes.

As with pasta it is advisable to refer to the manufacturer's recipe book but a guide as to the quantity of water to rice would be about one cup of rice to two cups of water.

The non-metallic container should be large enough to accommodate the rice and water with ease and it should be covered during the cooking process but not so tightly that steam cannot escape.

In general, quick cooking rice is put into boiling water whereas the conventional rice is put into cold water. As to be expected the rice which is put into cold water would take longer to cook as the water also has to be heated. Nevertheless, whichever type of rice is being cooked it must always be left to stand in the covered container after the cooking operation for seven to ten minutes. After the standing period, the rice should be fluffed up with a fork before serving and if desired reheated.

The method of reheating rice is exactly the same as would be used for pasta.

Should rice dishes be frozen these may be thawed in a covered container, the rice being placed in the oven for about 5 minutes for a 300 gram (10 oz.) quantity, at which point the rice should be broken up and stirred. It is then returned to the oven for a further period of two minutes, stirred once again and left to stand covered for approximately two minutes before serving.

Cereals which are invariably eaten at breakfast time can be quickly and easily made as and when required in the individual uncovered non-metallic cereal dish. The cereal is put into the dish and the liquid stirred in. All that is then necessary is about a minute or two's cooking in the oven, another stir and then it should be ready to eat. If larger quantities are required then a large non-metallic uncovered container should be used and the cereal should be stirred once or twice during the cooking operation.

Puddings and desserts The range of puddings and desserts which may be cooked in a microwave oven is extensive and almost endless. The microwave oven manufacturer's recipe book always seems to give a very large variety and these include both hot and cold puddings and desserts. However, as with the case of most foods the conventional brown colour cannot be achieved but in the majority of cases the dish itself will have sufficient colour to make it acceptable. As the range is so extensive it includes dishes such as upside down cakes, bread puddings, fruit crumbles and dumplings, cheese cakes, suet puddings, crême caramels and mousses, consequently it would be difficult to specify broad principles as to the shape, size and covering requirements for a container. Therefore, it can only be said that if the moisture in the food needs to be retained then it would be likely that the container should be covered. In addition, it is also possible that the user may be able to use the same dish in which the food has been cooked to serve to table.

The thawing of frozen desserts and puddings is simple, following the principle of giving the food short bursts of microwave energy followed by a standing period to allow the heat within the food to continue the thawing process during the standing period.

A further advantage is that of reheating, so often a pudding or dessert is made one day and eaten the next but the beauty of a microwave oven is its ability to allow the user to reheat the mass or to serve either hot or cold individual portions depending upon the family's preference.

Soups Soups can be made in the microwave oven from fresh ingredients, tinned soups can be reheated, or dehydrated soups reconstituted and reheated, and as to be expected frozen soups may be thawed and reheated with little or no effort. The uncovered non-metallic container should be large enough to contain the liquid should boiling occur and the soup should be stirred once or twice during the heating period. Very often it is quicker to heat the soup in the serving dishes or mugs and serve straight to the table, but there is no reason why the soup should not be heated in a non-metallic tureen and served from this. The heating time of the soup will depend upon the initial temperature of the soup and the size of the container, but it is only a question of a few minutes. When heating dehydrated soups they should be left to stand for about 5 minutes before serving, but as there are so many types on the market it is worth experimenting. Nevertheless, it is likely that in this instance the conventional method of heating would be preferred. To thaw soups an uncovered non-metallic container is used and during the

30

operation the soup should be broken up with a fork and stirred occasionally. The time taken would be dependent upon the type and quantity of the soup but the time would only be in the region of a few minutes.

Sauces These are both simple and quick to make in the microwave oven and there is little chance of burning or scorching them. In addition, sauces which have been cooked the day before and refrigerated may be quickly reheated for serving or frozen sauces can be thawed and reheated in no time at all.

The range of sauces is extensive covering the conventional to the exotic. Because sauce making is so simple in a microwave oven it is likely that sauces will be made to accompany dishes more than ever before, especially as the sauce can be made in the container in which it is to be served. Once again, it is advisable, especially during the period of getting to know the microwave oven, not to overcook the sauce because cooking continues a few minutes after it has been removed from the oven.

The container in which the sauce is made should be large enough to contain the liquid should boiling occur, and the cooking operation is carried out with the container uncovered. Some examples of simplicity of sauce making in a microwave oven are: *chocolate sauce* where melted chocolate, water, syrup and evaporated milk can be combined together before placing in the oven. *Jam sauce* some jam with a little water heated together: *quick caramel sauce* caramel sweets melted in the oven produce the desired result. The choice is endless, but perhaps the basic sauce that is likely to be used most frequently is a white sauce. The operation is simple, the butter is melted in a container in the microwave oven, after which, when flour and milk are blended in, it is just a question of cooking for about 3 minutes and giving a stir about every minute for 250 ml ($\frac{1}{2}$ pint approx.).

To thaw frozen sauces a covered non-metallic container is used and the same procedure as used to thaw soups would be employed.

Vegetables Most vegetables whether they be tinned, frozen or fresh can be thawed, reheated or cooked quickly in a microwave oven and, apart from the speed and convenience, the vegetables themselves tend to retain their vivid colour, specific flavours, and nutrients. In addition to which little if any water is used, and as a result the serving of soggy vegetables is a thing of the past. So far as frozen vegetables are concerned it is unlikely that any extra water is required as there will be a sufficient quantity available once the ice has melted. Tinned vegetables do not require all the liquor in which they are tinned and most of this should be poured off before heating the vegetables. An indication as to the quantities required is given in Table 2 but it should be noted that it is only intended as a guide and the individual manufacturer's recipe book should be referred to.

Table 2. **Water requirements for fresh vegetables**

Vegetable	Quantity	Water
Artichokes	4 medium	375 ml (12 fl.oz approx.)
Asparagus	12 stalks	75 ml (3 fl.oz approx.)
Runner beans	500 grams (1 lb approx.)	75 ml (3 fl.oz. approx.)
Beetroots	4 medium	Cover with water
Broccoli	500 grams (1 lb approx.)	75 ml (3 fl.oz approx.)
Brussels sprouts	500 grams (1 lb approx.)	40 ml (1½ fl.oz approx.)
Cabbage	1 medium	75 ml (3 fl.oz approx.)
Carrots	6 medium	75 ml (3 fl.oz approx.)
Cauliflower	1 medium	40 ml (1½ fl.oz approx.)
Aubergine	500 grams (1 lb approx.)	75 ml (3 fl.oz approx.)
Mushrooms	500 grams (1 lb approx.)	40 ml (1½ fl.oz approx.)
Small onions	500 grams (1 lb approx.)	None
Parsnips	4 medium	75 ml (3 fl.oz approx.)
Peas	1 kg (2 lb approx.)	40 ml (1½ fl.oz approx.)
Potatoes (boiled)	Any quantity	Cover with water
Spinach	500 grams (1 lb approx.)	With water that clings to the leaves

All vegetables, whether they be fresh, frozen or tinned will heat and cook more evenly when covered and it is therefore advisable to always cover the non-metallic container but not so tightly that the steam is unable to escape. It is also recommended that they should be stirred at least once during the operation but even more important they should not be overcooked as they quickly dehydrate and become tough as a result. This is particularly the case with vegetables having a high starch content. The addition of salt when cooking vegetables in the conventional manner is normal practice, but to put salt over vegetables when heating or cooking by microwaves tends to dehydrate them. Therefore, any salt should be put in the bottom of the container rather than sprinkled over the vegetables themselves and the benefit of the salt will reach all the vegetables as they are stirred during the cooking operation.

Frozen vegetables may be defrosted and cooked in one operation and tinned vegetables simply reheated. However, it is difficult to be specific as to the cooking time of vegetables as their age, freshness and quality can have a bearing on the cooking time. Nevertheless, the following Tables 3 and 4 are a guide as to the sort of times which could be expected.

Table 3. **Cooking and Heating Guide**

Product	Quantity	Application	Preparation	Water added	Stir/ shake	Time
Apple sauce	6	Cooking	Peel, core and cut	Yes	Yes	8 min
Beans (green)	10 oz (300 g)	Cooking	Cut in small pieces—cook	Yes	Yes	10 min
Beans (green)	14 oz (450 g)	Heating	Open can	Yes	Yes	4 min
Broccoli	8 oz (250 g)	Heating	Heat—covered	No	Yes	2½ min
Broccoli	8 oz (250 g)	Cooking	Cook—wrapped in cellophane	No	Yes	9 min
Brussels sprouts	16 oz (500 g)	Cooking	Clean, cook—covered	Yes	Yes	12 min
Brussels sprouts	7 oz (200 g)	Heating	Heat—covered	No	Yes	5 min
Cabbage (white)	16 oz (500 g)	Cooking	Cut and cook—covered	Yes	Yes	12 min
Cabbage (white)	16 oz (500 g)	Heating	Heat—covered	No	Yes	6 min
Carrots	14 oz (450 g)	Cooking	Cut in slices, cook—covered	Yes	Yes	14 min
Carrots	14 oz (450 g)	Heating	Heat—covered	No	Yes	4 min
Cauliflower	14 oz (450 g)	Cooking	Make roses, cook—covered	Yes	Yes	15 min
Cauliflower	14 oz (450 g)	Heating	Heat—covered	No	Yes	3 min
Celery	10 oz (300 g)	Heating	Heat—covered	No	Yes	4 min
Chicory	10 oz (300 g)	Cooking	Cook—covered	Yes	Yes	11 min
Chicory	10 oz (300 g)	Heating	Heat—covered	No	Yes	4 min
Corn-on-the-cob	1	Cooking	Cook wrapped in cellophane	Yes	No	7 min
Corn (cut)	12 oz (350 g)	Heating	Heat—covered	No	Yes	3 min
Cucumber	10 oz (300 g)	Cooking	Peel, cut in pieces, cook—covered	Yes	Yes	5 min
Leeks	16 oz (500 g)	Cooking	Cut thinly, cook—covered	Yes	Yes	15 min
Peas	14 oz (450 g)	Heating	Heat—covered	Yes	Yes	3½ min

Continued overleaf

Table 3 (cont'd)

Product	Quantity	Application	Preparation	Water added	Stir/ shake	Time
Potatoes	16 oz (500 g)	Cooking	Peel, cut, cook—covered	Yes	Yes	15 min
Spinach	16 oz (500 g)	Cooking	Cook—covered with water that clings to the leaves	No	Yes	7 min
Sweet pepper	2 halves	Cooking	Cook—covered	Yes	Yes	5 min
Miscellaneous						
3 component meal	16 oz (500g)	Heating	Heat—covered	No	Yes	4½ min
Soup	1 cup	Heating	Heat—uncovered	No	Yes	90 sec
Milk	1 glass	Heating	Heat—uncovered	No	Yes	30/40sec
Chocolate	1 glass	Heating	Mix ingredients, heat uncovered	No	Yes	90 sec
Coffee/tea	1 cup	Heating	Boil water add coffee or tea	No	Yes	1½ min
Ragoûts/stews	8 oz (250 g)	Heating	Heat—covered	No	Yes	3 min
Rice	16 oz (500 g)	Heating	Heat—covered	No	Yes	4 min
Mashed potatoes	14 oz (450 g)	Heating	Heat—covered	No	Yes	5 min

Chart provided by kind permission of Philips Electrical Limited.

Table 4. **Frozen Food Cooking Guide**

Food	Quantity	Application	Preparation	Water added	Stir/ shake/ turn	Time
Apple sauce	14 oz (450 g)	Defrosting	Heat—uncovered	No	Yes	10 min
Beans (green)	10 oz (300g)	Defrosting + cooking	Small pieces wrapped in cellophane, cook—covered	Yes	Yes	12 min
Broccoli	10 oz (300 g)	Defrosting + cooking	Wrap in cellophane cook–covered	Yes	Yes	12 min
Brussels sprouts	7 oz (175 g)	Defrosting + cooking	Cook—covered	Yes	Yes	9 min
Cabbage	14 oz (450 g)	Defrosting + cooking	Cook—covered	No	Yes	12 min
Carrots	10 oz (300 g)	Defrosting + cooking	Cook—covered	Yes	Yes	14 min
Cauliflower	14 oz (450 g)	Defrosting + cooking	Cook—covered	Yes	Yes	12 min
Corn	13 oz (425 g)	Defrosting + cooking	Cook—covered	Yes	Yes	11 min
Mixed vegetables	8 oz (250 g)	Defrosting + cooking	Cook—covered	Yes	Yes	9 min
Peas	8 oz (250 g)	Defrosting + cooking	Cook—covered	Yes	Yes	9 min
Peas and carrots	8 oz (250 g)	Defrosting + cooking	Cook—covered	Yes	Yes	9 min
Spinach	13 oz (425 g)	Defrosting + cooking	Cook—covered	Yes	Yes	8 min
Miscellaneous						
Bread, slice		Defrosting	Uncovered	No	No	30 sec
Bread, loaf		Defrosting with intervals	Uncovered	No	Yes	3 min

Table 4 (cont'd)

Food	Quantity	Application	Preparation	Water added	Stir/ shake/ turn	Time
Cake, slice		Defrosting	Uncovered	No	No	40 sec
Fruits	14 oz (450 g)	Defrosting with intervals	Uncovered	No	Yes	8 min
Mashed potatoes	16 oz (500 g)	Defrosting + heating	Covered	No	Yes	9 min
Chicken ragoût	15 oz (475 g)	Defrosting	Covered	No	Yes	10 min
Complete meals	16 oz (500 g)	Defrosting + heating	Covered	No	Yes	7–10 min
Rice	16 oz (500 g)	Defrosting + heating	Covered	No	Yes	10 min

Chart provided by kind permission of Philips Electrical Limited.

Should any vegetable be cooked within its skin, the skin should be pierced to prevent the vegetable from bursting during the cooking operation. Certainly, potatoes in their jackets are one of the popular microwave vegetables as they can literally be cooked in minutes and are simply prepared by scrubbing and pricking them, arranging them on absorbent paper allowing a space between each and turning them around half way during the cooking period.

Blanching for the freezer It is possible to carry out blanching in the microwave oven. The preparation of vegetables both before and after blanching remains the same but the quantity of water used is very much less, only about 75 ml (3 fl. oz) to 500 g (1 lb) of vegetables. The vegetables and water are placed in a large covered container and cooked for approximately 4–6 minutes, but it is important (a) to stir or turn the food once during the operation, (b) give a standing time of 1 minute before cooling in ice water, (c) not to overcook as the vegetables would be less sweet and more starchy, (d) to blanch small quantities at a time.

CHAPTER 3
Tips for the microwave oven user

The various chapters in this book endeavour to cover the basic information which may be required by a prospective or new user. However, this chapter is not only intended to condense some of this data but to give further information as to how the microwave oven can be manipulated to fit in with the individual's own requirements.

The new user of a microwave oven can be forgiven if she does not initially use the appliance to the full. Certainly, for the first month she may even ponder as to why it was purchased in the beginning. Nevertheless, suddenly it will become an appliance as indispensable as the refrigerator or washing machine. Furthermore, some may feel guilty if the microwave oven is not used as the only appliance in the kitchen. However, it is worth remembering that in general, and this is accepted by most, although a basic microwave oven unit will take over in many instances it is also highly successful, perhaps even more so, when used in conjunction with other kitchen appliances.

Adaptability is perhaps the key word when used in conjunction with a microwave oven as it is not just an oven in the true sense of the word. Thus, as its applications are many, it may be necessary, initially, to think twice before using a conventional piece of equipment, as it is more than likely that the microwave oven will be able to carry out the same operation but with more speed, less inconvenience and possibly more cheaply.

For those on special diets, whether they be self imposed or under medical direction, the microwave oven may prove to be more than useful. Special food preferences can be accommodated with the minimum of effort. Left over foods or complete meals can be quickly and easily reheated. Hot food can be produced at any time of the day or night, and almost anyone can operate the oven without too much tuition. Naturally, there are many other uses for the microwave oven, but often it is the actual user who finally decides as to which of its many attributes is the most important one for her.

Tips for the microwave oven user can be listed but perhaps the best tip of all is that of experimenting. Everyone is an individual and as such will have both favourite recipes and methods of working. Thus, if the general principles are observed the microwave oven will adapt to the user as it is she who will be in control with regard to time, stirring, rotating containers, and opening the door at will.

Should the oven be of the type which must not be operated without a food load it is a good idea to always stand a cup or glass of water in the oven so that should anyone switch on accidentally no damage to the magnetron could occur.

At no time should metal containers or foil be used in a microwave oven. The only exception would be if the microwave oven manufacturer specifically states that it is possible.

The uses to which a microwave oven may be put seem to be endless and the suggestions made by the microwave oven manufacturers are very useful, although it is likely that some of the operations would not be carried out every day. These include warming a baby's bottle, warming lotion or baby oil, drying flowers for pot pourri, drying wet newspapers, removing the stamps from envelopes and even curling false eyelashes. Although interesting, these functions are not going to be the main reason for having a microwave oven. And indeed as an appliance it is able to carry out other quick operations which will be of rather more benefit. Melting chocolate can be done in a bowl, without the need of pans, hot water, and the worry of over-cooking; butter can be softened for both spreading and cooking; small quantities of fats can be melted to be used for brushing foods, making cakes, or making sauces. Cubes of bread can be dried ready for stuffings; frozen or refrigerated icings and frostings may be easily softened ready for use; milk can be scalded; grapefruits baked in minutes; canapés for cocktails and parties heated as required and herbs dried. All of these are not particularly spectacular, but when working in a conventional kitchen these are the sort of jobs which can prove to be inconvenient and time consuming.

Soufflés and egg custards may be cooked successfully in some ovens where the microwave energy can be reduced. However, should this facility not be available, success can frequently be achieved if the container holding the mixture is placed in a further container containing water. This extra moisture within the oven appears to benefit the egg mixture.

Milk or milk based soups, sauces etc., have a tendency to 'boil over', therefore it is wise to use a container large enough to prevent 'boiling over' occurring.

Whole foods such as tomatoes, apples, jacket potatoes will all cook well but the skins should always be either pricked or slit to enable the steam within the food to escape. Should this not be done the skin will burst and the shape lost. In addition to which, in bursting, the contents may splatter and as a result incur an unnecessary cleaning operation. This principle would apply to any food having a skin or membrane.

Tough meats are unlikely to become tender when cooked in a microwave oven as the microwaves do cook food very quickly. Thus, in some instances, for example when stewing, the conventional methods of cooking will possibly be preferred. However, if an oven has a very low output this would not necessarily be the case as longer slower cooking could be achieved.

As with conventional cooking, extra cooking time should be given to stuffed meat and poultry—this could be in the region of an extra 5 minutes to the pound.

In general microwave ovens cannot brown foods because the surface temperature of the food will not exceed 100°C (212°F) whilst water is present. However, this is unimportant where the foods themselves have a colour such as vegetables, fruits, flavoured cakes, casseroles or those foods which are to be covered in a sauce. Nevertheless, there will be certain occasions where a brown colour is required. In these instances it is possible to utilise a preheated grill to 'flash' the food and this would answer the specific need without losing the benefits of microwave cooking. But the answer may also be found in the oven itself by inserting large joints or poultry in a roasting bag or by using a browning dish.

In certain circumstances small pieces of meat and poultry can achieve a fairly attractive appearance if they are brushed with unsalted butter before the cooking operation.

Seasoning should be used sparingly and adjusted according to taste at the completion of the operation. Salt should never be sprinkled directly onto food such as meat or vegetables as this absorbs moisture and as a result can toughen the food.

Eggs in shells cannot be cooked in the oven and it is inadvisable to try any form of experiment as the shell could shatter and cause damage to the oven.

Several foods can be cooked in the oven at the same time but it is wise to check that one item has not heated or cooked before another. If one is ready, then it should be removed to prevent it from dehydrating.

Unlike conventional oven cooking the microwave oven door in general can be opened as frequently as desired without causing detriment to the food being cooked.

When thawing foods, the operation can be speeded up if the half thawed food is gently broken up with a fork, and any large pieces of ice removed from the container.

The containers do remain relatively cool especially if compared to those employed for conventional cooking. Nevertheless, sometimes they can get fairly hot as a result of the high temperatures reached by the food. In addition, where foods have been covered, the cover or covering should be removed with care to avoid any steam from causing inconvenience.

To save the tiresome chore of washing up unnecessary dishes it is an advantage to make full use of non-metallic tableware by getting into the habit of cooking and serving with it.

Foods cook more evenly if they are of an even depth, therefore with foods that can be arranged in this way, e.g. vegetables, casseroles and the like, it is better to arrange them spread out over a larger container rather than piled into a smaller one.

Food is very, very hot when it is removed from the oven therefore, if tasting for seasoning, allow the food to cool in a spoon before taking it to the mouth.

Most foods will be successfully reheated in a microwave oven but in certain instances the result may be unacceptable. Examples of these would be fried chipped potatoes or foods which have been cooked in batter. The process of heating is successful—the food is piping hot, but due to the moisture created during the process the crisp exterior becomes limp and consequently less palatable.

Although small amounts of butter, etc., may be melted in the microwave oven shallow or deep frying must not be attempted.

The oven will keep very clean but should any food splatter or be spilt it is better to wipe up the soil immediately as the food will continue to enjoy the benefit of the microwave energy even though it is not in the container.

Foil, used in small quantities is useful to 'shield' the food but must only be used if recommended by the manufacturer. If it can be employed, then be sure to avoid it touching any of the oven walls as this can sometimes cause 'arcing' and in turn damage the magnetron. To secure the foil, a wooden cocktail stick can be a useful means of anchoring it.

Sometimes it is quicker and less energy is used if a conventional appliance is employed rather than the microwave oven. This is likely to be the case in boiling water if an electric kettle is a part of the kitchen. In general, the kettle element will be in direct contact with the water and consequently will heat and boil it very quickly. Therefore, if more than 500ml (1 pint) of hot or boiling water is required the electric kettle may prove to be a more efficient and convenient appliance to use.

It is possible that a microwave oven owner may wish to purchase an optional extra item available with another manufacturer's microwave oven. However, it is unwise to use any extra items without having first consulted the manufacturer of your own microwave oven. The reason is that optional extras are frequently designed with the oven itself and if used in another oven, success may not be achieved or damage to the oven itself could be incurred.

Instruction and recipe books are supplied by the microwave oven manufacturers but should further microwave oven books be used it must be remembered that because the features and energy outputs could be different from oven to oven, then both the procedures and cooking times may have to be adjusted accordingly to achieve the desired results. In addition, it is inadvisable to carry out any operation which is contrary to the microwave oven manufacturer's instructions.

People who are familiar with microwave ovens will use a vocabulary which may be new to many and a number of these terms and expressions, e.g. 'standing time', 'resting period', 'equalizing' have been used and explained in the various chapters of this book. However, it is important to the user not to be 'blinded by science' or 'put off'. Thus, should any expressions be used in the microwave world which are unfamiliar, it is well worth while asking for an explanation, as frequently the explanation will lead to a better way of using the oven.

A better height of rise of a cake is frequently achieved if the made uncooked mixture is left to stand for 3–4 minutes before cooking, as this gives the raising agent the opportunity to become more active.

CHAPTER 4
The use of microwave in catering

Although a great deal has been said about the domestic applications of the microwave oven, it should not be forgotten that like so many other domestic appliances the original concept started in the catering industry and was (and is) used very successfully before its success and benefits permeated to the domestic front.

Philips 2 kW microwave oven model 2010C

Every caterer is an individual as is every customer and each must be treated as such. Nevertheless, the needs of the individual caterer can be discussed in terms of numbers, whereas the customer can only think of himself as an individual having his needs and desires catered for at that immediate moment. It is expected and taken for granted that the caterer will provide a service, yet he could have a multitude of problems to contend with behind the scenes and even these circumstances could change almost over night.

There could be willing staff, but they may not necessarily be conversant with the language. The customer demand may be spasmodic or regular. There may be added difficulties, in so much that the business is very successful, but because of lack of space and inflexible equipment, continual harrassment is the order of the day. In addition to which, a profit must be made whether it be for an individual or for an organisation. These and many more problems beset the caterer and at this point it could be questioned as to how the use of a microwave oven would be of benefit to him.

So far as the benefits of a microwave oven are concerned much of what has been said in other chapters of this book will relate to the caterer. Nevertheless, commercial microwave ovens cannot be regarded in exactly the same way. Two immediate examples of this would be that of the saving of time and the choice of menu. A saving of time is very useful to the home user, but this is well and truly magnified when the commercial need is applied, as within this environment the caterer is not only having to deal with the individual, but could within the same moment in time, have to give a service to vast numbers of people. In addition to which, unlike the home user, it is difficult for him to be precise as to the exact hour that the service will be demanded. So far as the menu is concerned, the home user makes a menu decision usually in advance and in general no choice is given. However, the caterer is often expected to give both an à la carte and a table d'hôte menu and the table d'hôte menu would be expected to include some sort of choice.

The commercial application

As the commercial needs in the area of the microwave oven are different to those required in the home the priorities change. Thus, prime cooking is of lesser importance but reheating and/or thawing of frozen foods becomes the most important requirement. The microwave oven has its limitations and because of its inability to brown and the need to cook very large quantities of foodstuffs the use of the conventional catering equipment for this type of cooking is probably more successful. Nevertheless, the speed at which foods can be thawed and reheated will give advantages in other directions. Thus, the microwave oven in the catering field may be successfully utilised to back up existing equipment and introduce further benefits. However, where catering is not considered to be 'large scale' the commercial microwave oven used as the sole cooking appliance can fulfil a need and make a profit. To briefly examine the benefits:

Thawing: Pre-cooked speciality dishes and foods may be purchased or made in advance and be stored in a freezer until demanded. Not only would this reduce food wastage but could introduce a more varied or exciting menu.

The 'gamble' of removing too much food from the freezer at the beginning of the day is lessened, thus the quantities could err on the low side with the knowledge that should more be necessary, thawing the product will only take a short time.

Reheating: Both speciality and everyday dishes may be reheated rapidly, therefore the risk of bacteria growth is greatly reduced due to the high temperature that food will attain in a very short time. Quickie foods such as rolls, pies, cornish pasties, frankfurters, etc., can be heated as and when ordered.

Hot foods can be supplied at any time of the day or night and be dealt with by a staff having no knowledge of food preparation.

Food which may or may not have been kept hot in a separate heating area may have its temperature boosted before serving.

Sauces can be reheated in any non-metallic container for table service.

Prime cooking: The microwave oven can be usefully employed to make some sauces either at the time requested or earlier in the day. Fish may be successfully thawed and cooked quickly, yet retaining its shape and flavour although the time element is vital to ensure a perfect result. Nevertheless, large quantities of fish could be stored in the freezer until the moment required, and for prime cooking, kippers, being of such an appetising colour, are ideal.

Vegetables which are not in great demand can be cooked at the time they are ordered thus introducing less wastage, and due to the high speed cooking greater vitamin retention can be achieved.

These benefits do not cover all those which the caterer can relate to, indeed, those caterers who are already using ovens as a part of their existing scheme are likely to be able to suggest even greater advantages. Nevertheless, those given do give an indication as to the areas in which the catering microwave oven can be usefully employed.

Siting the microwave oven

As in the case of domestic microwave ovens, the commercial microwave oven may be sited almost anywhere where it is going to be convenient. This could be part of the back bar equipment, on a table, built into a unit, or placed in some convenient corner of a kitchen or room. In addition to which it is of such a size that it may be used and moved almost at will without unnecessary loss of time, effort and money. Indeed its weight is taken for granted, but if a comparison was made between the first microwave oven sold in 1959 where it was so heavy that it took some four men to move it, then perhaps this feature would be appreciated even more. Weights of microwave ovens can be as low as 27 kg, for example a smaller domestic model, and as high as 75 kg for a commercial model.

Due to the specific needs of the catering environment the

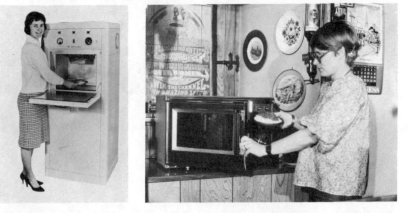

A 1959 catering microwave oven
Photograph by *R. Constable*

A 1977 catering microwave oven
Litton Microwave Cooking Products

45

microwave wattage of the commercial oven can be higher than those obtained for the domestic market and in this instance it may be necessary to have fixed wiring. Nevertheless, the vast majority of the commercial microwave ovens do not need special wiring and may be simply plugged into a $2 \cdot 5$ mm^2 (13 or 15 amp) socket outlet.

Types of containers

The types of containers and dishes which may be used are extensive and the principles given in Chapter 7 of this book would still apply. However, food suppliers who supply both refrigerated, frozen dishes and complete meals are very aware of the convenience of having foods accommodated in and on the type of containers which may be used in the microwave oven. Thus, the caterer may in addition to using his own kitchen utensils, dishes and service ware also utilise the benefit given by his food supplier. Consequently less washing up is required and a quick easy service is maintained.

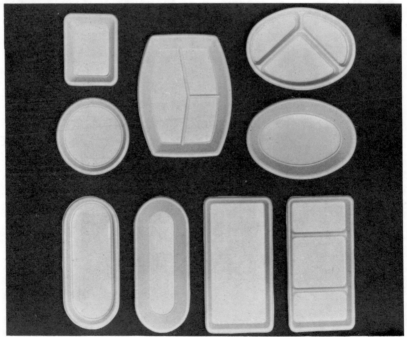

A selection of microwave oven trays. *Formpak Limited*

Where and how microwave ovens are used

Microwave ovens have been used in various operations, some of which have proved to be more successful than others. Nevertheless, the versatility of microwave has and does introduce new ideas and advantages for both the caterer and customer alike. A system has been employed where a customer selected a meal from a refrigerated unit, carried it to a table in the restaurant, and reheated it at his leisure. A similar system designed for the factory and office worker was by putting a coin in a slot, selecting a meal which would then automatically be conveyed through a microwave oven to the point where the customer would simply collect it. Both ideas, in principle, have potential; however, leading on from this concept there is a system widely used called the Microwave-Visi-Vend. This is a combination vending unit which is in use in big organisations such as hospitals and the Bank of England, where staff need to be able to obtain a hot meal at any time of the day or night. The unit itself comprises a refrigerated cabinet approximately 1·8 metres high (6 ft.) which accommodates 10 stacked turntables, and each turntable holds 10 trays of a selection of plated meals. A microwave oven unit is housed next to it and nearby the appropriate vending machines for desserts and drinks.

The customer simply places the appropriate money in a slot and then selects the meal required. Each meal comes complete with a serrated disc, the serrations representing a pre-determined timing device. The meal is then inserted into the microwave oven and the disc pushed into a slot. The meal is automatically given the correct heating time and within a short time it is piping hot and ready to eat. However, to give freedom of movement to the customer during the short waiting time the customer may select a dessert or obtain a hot drink to complete the meal and avoid 'hanging around'.

Microwave ovens will not only be found in restaurants, hotels, and hospitals, but behind bars in pubs, in local clubs, in staff rooms, take-away shops, offices, factories, schools, and indeed almost anywhere where space is limited and a service is demanded. Needless to say their versatility extends to both the sea and air. This even includes the Boeing 747 'Jumbo Jets', where the 28 first class passengers frequently enjoy a hot entrée

47

heated in the microwave oven installed in the galley.

The Mealstream System

The purpose of this book is to discuss microwave ovens on both the domestic and catering front, but it would be remiss not to take into consideration a further development.

The Mealstream System could be considered to be the alternative method of using microwave energy in the catering environment, but it must be called a cooker being primarily designed and constructed to replace the conventional type of cooker, or to compliment existing equipment in the kitchen. The Mealstream System adds to the basic microwave unit by incorporating heating elements and a fan in the oven, thus introducing hot air. Unlike the basic microwave oven it is larger and heavier and as a result does require more space and fixed wiring. Nevertheless, because its design has been extended, it is able to allow the chef to continue with his traditional methods of food preparation and service yet, due to the microwave speed, decrease the frustrations which can be encountered in a busy kitchen with continual pressure. The advantages gained by using microwave ovens have been fully covered in other chapters and these are still retained, but as the Mealstream cooker incorporates a fan and heating element the basic food cooking techniques such as roasting, baking, grilling, shallow frying and

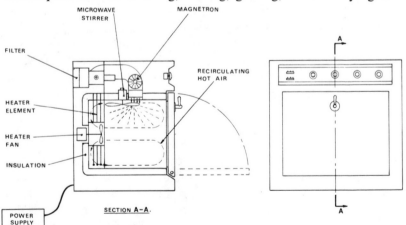

Figure 9. **The basic Mealstream cooker**

48

braising can be carried out completely thus dispensing with the need for auxilliary equipment such as grills.

The Mealstream Controls

As the oven is constructed with forced air convection as well as microwave it is possible to utilise microwave and forced air heat together, or separately to use only the forced air heat or microwave energy. For the vast majority of operations hot air and microwave are used simultaneously.

The control for the microwave energy is in dial form and a choice of energy from 500 Watts to 2·2 kW may be selected. The forced air control dial gives intermediate settings between 100°C (212°F) and 350°C (660°F). The dial timer control gives similar facilities to those found on conventional microwave ovens giving 0–5 minutes with 15 second graduations and from 6–35 minutes with minute graduations. A further control is incorporated on the facia, and this is for thawing or certain cooking operations which benefit by 'pulsed' microwave energy. In addition, indicator lights are fitted to complement the various controls.

Containers in the Mealstream

Due to the particular design of the cooker it is not only able to accommodate china, glass, paper, certain plastics, etc., but also metal whether it be iron, copper, aluminium, silver and such like, and the only exception in this instance would be that of using high sided metal utensils and metal lids. This acceptance of metal pans is essential to the extension of the cooker's range to cover all the basic cooking processes. The best results, however, are obtained, particularly in a busy catering kitchen, by starting with very hot pans those processes which traditionally require this approach. The full value of the hot air is used on the food rather than on heating cold metal. In which case, the utensils may be kept hot or warm on an existing hob unit within the kitchen. If required, however, the cooker may be purchased with a side hob to accommodate the various pans in use.

Nevertheless, it could be questioned as to how and why this cooker is able to accommodate metal whereas the basic microwave oven is unable to do so. The easiest analogy to make is with a camera. An inexpensive instant camera takes excellent

The galley on a British Rail High Speed Train. *British Rail.*

photographs but the best result is only obtained if the distance is correct—not too far and not too close. A more expensive instant camera has a lens which will automatically focus and consequently a better photograph will be produced.

The magnetron in the Mealstream accepts in very much the same way a change in focus, that is to say the apparent change in depth of the oven when metal pans effectively become a new, higher oven floor. As a result of this ability to accommodate alterations in the model characteristics of the oven cavity the magnetron is safeguarded against reflections which might otherwise damage it.

Like the basic microwave oven the Mealstream System can be found in many catering establishments both on land and sea, but its latest environment is that of the British Rail High Speed Trains.

CHAPTER 5
Nutritional aspects

Nutrition in itself is a very wide and complex subject but it is one which appears to create some interest when the subject of microwave ovens is mentioned. Although investigations have been carried out in the United Kingdom it would seem that very few papers have been published on the subject, but this is possibly due to the fact that a considerable amount of work has been carried out in the United States of America and from this area various publications are available. This would be quite feasible bearing in mind that the whole concept of microwave cooking started in the USA long before many other countries utilised this particular form of energy for cooking. However, much of the information relates to the use of microwave ovens in large scale catering environments such as schools, hospitals and so on. Nevertheless, the findings can, in many instances, be related to the domestic situation where similar methods of cooking are employed.

It is common knowledge that the nutritive value of foods can change under different types of storage conditions, food preparation, and during the cooking process. In addition to which, the extent of the losses will be influenced even further by the person who is preparing and cooking the food rather than any appliance which is being utilised for preparation and cooking purposes. So far as laboratory tests are concerned many of these variables can be ruled out to ensure that the results are factual, but as to be expected it is difficult to standardise on many of the natural foodstuffs. Thus, it is possible that when comparing nutrient retention figures they may not correlate exactly with those presented from other sources. Nevertheless, the overall picture is indicative of the various aspects of nutrient retention.

The aspect which seems to be the first which comes to mind is that of whether or not microwave cooking reduces or changes the nutritive value of food and, if so, is it more or less than would be found in conventional cooking? In general cooking in a microwave oven compares very favourably with conventional cooking methods and microwaves do not appear to be more harmful to nutrients. Indeed, nutrient retention can in many instances be greater when using a microwave oven providing that like conventional cooking the correct methods are used. It is an accepted fact that if vegetables are cooked with the minimum of water a greater nutrient retention can be achieved, this being especially the case with ascorbic acid, thiamin and riboflavin as all of these have a tendency to leach into liquid during the cooking process. As very little (if any) water is required when cooking vegetables in a microwave oven it is natural that these nutrients in particular will be retained.

Reheating food is another aspect to be considered as under normal reheating conditions the nutritive value of food can be reduced, this being especially so where extended reheating is carried out. The microwave oven can reduce this type of unnecessary loss mainly due to the ability of the oven to heat food very quickly, thus ensuring the retention of those nutrients which would normally be lost during conventional reheating methods.

As with all foods it is the appearance which will initially tempt the appetite but it would seem that very little work has been conducted in this area. Nevertheless, if the opinion of the microwave oven user is sought they will generally agree that the colour of food is greatly improved if microwave energy has been used as the heating or cooking method.

This is particularly the case where the food itself has strong natural pigments such as the green of peas and beans, the reds of tomatoes and plums, and the clear strong colour of orange in carrots, to name but a few. Of course, as mentioned in other chapters, when it comes to the appearance of certain foods the microwave oven does have some limitations, but outside of these the new brilliance and intensity of the natural pigments adds greater eye appeal to the many foods which can be cooked in the microwave oven.

The 'fresh' look of foods is paralleled by the flavour and the 'fresh' taste is an added experience. Here again it would seem that there is little documented evidence of this but many microwave oven users would be likely to agree the point. It is possible that the flavour could be attributed to the cooking method because as the food is cooked so very quickly in a microwave oven there is less loss of flavour, but whatever the reason the flavours in such foods as fish, meat, fruit and vegetables all take on a new meaning to the palate.

Nevertheless, in those areas where texture may contribute to the idea of flavour, such as with a crusty loaf, then the consumer may feel that the flavour is a new one and forget that the chemical reaction between the food sugars and amino acids would not necessarily be the same as would be found in the conventional roasting and baking operations.

On the whole it would appear that although there is quite a lot of documentation available, especially in the area of nutrient retention and vegetables, there is still plenty of scope for further work. However, the information which is available indicates that nutrient retention and improved colours and flavours are very much a part of cooking with microwaves.

CHAPTER 6

The features of a microwave oven

Looking at a row of microwave ovens tends to be something like looking at a row of television sets—apparently they are all the same and yet each, when examined more closely and in detail, offers some benefit or feature which could give even better results or better viewing.

The features on microwave ovens are many and consequently each is worth examining. As with most appliances some are basic and others give added versatility. Nevertheless, it is only the prospective user who can decide what will suit and meet his individual needs and requirements. Some features are optional extras and this could be a particular advantage to a new user who may wish to become familiar with the basic microwave oven before embarking on additional costs which may, in the event, prove to be unnecessary. The demand for microwave ovens is increasing at a very high rate and as would be expected both the features and designs are changing at the same speed, therefore it is possible that some of the features mentioned in this section will not be available for some time, but to be aware of such possibilities gives food for thought.

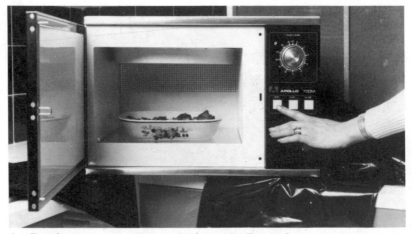

Apollo microwave oven model 700M. *Apollo Enterprises*

The controls

The simplest controls on a microwave oven could be in the form of a timer and a 'cook' button or switch. In which case, the user would simply place the food in the oven, set the timer for the 'cooking' time required, and start the microwave energy by pushing or switching on the 'cook' control. The oven would continue to produce the microwave energy until the timer had moved round to the 'off' position and then it would automatically switch off the microwave energy.

Should the user wish to gain access to the oven during the selected time the door may be opened but the action of the door opening would immediately switch off the microwave energy, and not until the door was closed and the 'cook' button or switch had been turned on would the microwave energy start again.

The timer could be either a clockwork or electric type, in which case it should be remembered that should the oven door be opened the clockwork timer would tick on regardless whereas the electric timer would automatically stop until the actual cooking operation had been re-started.

This would be a very basic oven although it should be noted that there could, in the future, be ovens which would only have a timer as a control. On the whole most ovens will incorporate extra buttons or switches as described below, they may be found in various combinations.

The timer control Most microwave ovens will have at least one timer and the maximum time which could be selected is unlikely to exceed 60 minutes but in general 30 minute timers are fitted. As seconds and minutes are used in microwave cooking it is usual for the minutes given at the lower end of the scale to be sub-divided in 10–15 second graduations, whereas at the higher end of the scale the second graduations increase to 30 seconds if given at all. The form of the control may be as a dial or sliding device but as accuracy in setting is an important requirement it is wise to ensure that the markings and method of alignment is clear and simple to set.

The 'cook' control The name implies that the control is for cooking only but this is not the case. The control is simply a device for switching the microwave energy on and it would not matter whether the user was thawing, heating or cooking. Generally it is in the form of a push button switch. However, on some appliances this control may be called the 'start' control.

The On/Off control Some microwave ovens have an On/Off control push button or switch. This control is used as an On/Off switch like many other electrical appliances but the operation of this switch on a microwave oven may also start the cooling fan and bring on the interior oven light. On some ovens when the control is operated there may be a very short delay period of about 10 seconds before the oven can be used. This is to allow the power source to warm up prior to use. Should this control not be visible on the oven it will be automatically operated when the oven is connected and switched on at the supply.

The 'Off' position An 'Off' position may be incorporated at the end of the timer which gives an indication that the cooking time has finished or may be a method of turning the oven light off. However, if a separate button or control is fitted this in general will operate in accordance with the methods as described in the On/Off control section.

The interior oven light control If an interior oven light is fitted, it generally illuminates as soon as the appliance is switched on. Some models may be provided with a separate switch, and at least one other model has the light interlocked with the 'cook' control.

The automatic defrost control As the microwave oven heats food so quickly it is necessary, when thawing frozen foods, to manually carry out the operation by subjecting the frozen product to the microwave energy in stages, e.g. 30 seconds using microwave energy, followed by a short 'rest' period and then repeating the process until the frozen food is evenly thawed. On some ovens however an automatic defrost control may be provided in the form of a button or dial, which may or may not work in conjunction with the timer. When operated it will automatically 'pulse' the microwave energy so that the user would not have to be in attendance during the process.

Power level control In general once the 'cook' control has been operated the microwave energy will remain constant and this allows the user to concentrate simply on time. However, a new innovation is where, by using a dial or slide control, a choice may be made of decreasing the microwave energy obtained thus introducing a 'slower' cooking rate. The method of marking this varies from manufacturer to manufacturer but may be in the form of words such as low, medium and high, or simmer, roast and reheat.

Toshiba ER766 microwave oven with variable power control

Wattage (input and output)

Most people are familiar with the term wattage and this relates to the electrical power supplied. To obtain the benefits of electrical power this has to be converted to a useful form which could be, to name a few, heat, light, motive power.

Some examples are:

A 1000 watt heater when connected to the electricity supply will give the user 1000 watts of heat.

A 100 watt light bulb when fitted into a lamp holder does give light but not 100 watts of it as some of the energy is in the form of heat. This can be illustrated by holding a hand near to a light bulb when it is on.

A 500 watt motor on a vacuum cleaner when connected to the electricity supply will give sufficient suction to pick up dust but not 500 watts as some of the energy is in the form of heat. Thus this is the reason why the air is warm when expelled from the non-suction end of a cleaner.

Therefore, the wattage stated on the appliance as the input and the output is what the useful wattage is in the form of, for instance, heat, light, or motive power. In general, many people assume that the output will be the same as the input regardless of the work it is designed to do but this is not one-hundred per cent correct.

As with all electrical appliances the microwave oven has a stated input (wattage) but confusion can occur because the manufacturer is likely to quote a figure for both input and output and these will not agree.

For example: the input for a microwave oven could be given as 1000 watts whereas the output may be stated as 500 watts. This is because some of the watts have been used to convert the electrical energy into microwaves. Thus, the 500 watts indicate the actual microwave energy available for thawing, heating and cooking.

Catering microwave ovens will usually have a greater output than domestic ovens because the user's needs are different. The catering microwave ovens may have outputs of anything between 600 and 2000 watts, whereas the domestic oven may be between 250 and 750 watts. However, the average domestic oven is likely to be in the region of between 500–700 watts and these outputs are those generally suited to the cooking requirements of the home user. However, it may be possible to obtain an oven with a choice of outputs which could then extend the range of cooking to those foods which would benefit from a slower cooking time. Nevertheless, it must be remembered that whatever time is taken to heat or cook foods in a microwave oven this will invariably be much shorter than the time taken by cooking with conventional methods.

Door handles and latches The variety is extensive as some ovens have handles and others do not, thus the method of door opening will vary from oven to oven. Door fastening could be either as a door latch on the door itself, a push button on the control panel or incorporated in the door handle design, and some ovens may not have a latch at all.

Indicator lights Indicator lights on any appliance can prove to be a useful benefit and there are microwave ovens available which incorporate one or more of these.

The function of an indicator light is to remind the user that a certain operation has been set, is in process or finished. These lights on microwave ovens can be used to indicate the appliance has been connected and switched on at the mains, that the 'cook' operation is in progress, or that the 'cook' operation has finished. It is possible that some models will have further indicator lights which the manufacturer considers to be relevant to his particular oven design, in which case, the user, as an individual must decide as to the convenience of these.

Audible reminders Many microwave oven timers incorporate an audible reminder which indicates when the 'cook' process has been completed. This is automatic and may be in the form of a bell or 'buzzer'. It may be one of three types: either as a single note, or as a continuous ring or buzz lasting for several seconds after the completion of the 'cook' period, or it may be maintained until the timer has been turned to the 'off' position.

Air filters Some microwave oven manufacturers incorporate an air filter in the appliance, which as the term implies is for filtering the air, and as with any filter it should be periodically checked and cleaned to ensure that it is free from any build up of grease and soil as this could impair the cooling of the internal components.

Oven doors The purpose of having a door on a conventional oven, apart from giving access to the oven is to complete a 'box' which is capable of retaining the heat within the area and thus cooking foods. Similarly, the microwave oven door is designed to prevent microwave energy leaking from the oven. Thus, very special care and attention is taken to ensure that the microwave oven door gives, when closed, the best seal possible. (See Chapter 1 *Security in Design*.) Nevertheless, even with all the foolproof design and care given nobody can account for a user who wilfully and intentionally abuses an appliance. Unlike conventional oven doors the microwave oven door uses either capacitor or choke type seals, thus it is of a specialised design and should be respected as such. To maintain the efficiency of the door seals, they must be kept free of soil by wiping with a soft damp cloth. Scouring pads or cleaners must *never* be used and should the door at any time not close properly, the oven should not be used until it has been repaired by the manufacturer's service department or authorised agent. The cleaning and care of the door is important, thus the manufacturer's instructions for cleaning and other routine maintenance should be followed.

The type of doors available on microwave ovens may be one of three designs: drop down, side opening or a flush fitting type which slides up. As to the convenience of these, the choice is really dependent on what the user prefers. However, whichever type of door opening is selected it should be remembered that the door is fitted for a specific purpose and is not intended to be used as a leaning post, a tea towel drying facility, a container supporting shelf, or a 'do it yourself' enthusiast's toy.

A door may be constructed of a solid piece of metal, a metal mesh, glass or plastics and a metal mesh. Should the door incorporate or be of a mesh type it is not possible for the microwaves to pass through any of the tiny holes and the microwaves will always be contained in the oven.

Merrychef 96 with slide-up door.

Cooking guide A panel is sometimes accommodated on the front of the appliance which enables the operator to see without referring to a book the basic information required for a 'cooking' operation. This, in principle, can be useful but it is advisable to check that the information given does relate to the type of cooking likely to be carried out in the user's home.

The oven cavity On the whole, it is not possible to readily obtain a microwave oven of the same size as a conventional oven, as its size is determined by the need to transfer the microwave energy efficiently into the food. Nevertheless, there is a choice, but it should be noted that the biggest may not necessarily be the best. A useful guide when comparing ovens is to consider the size in relation to the size of containers which are likely to be used. In addition, although the oven cavity may appear to be small it can accommodate such items as a good size Christmas turkey or joint which will be of benefit to many. Although not related to the size of the oven a point to be aware of is that some microwave ovens must not be switched on unless there is a food load within the oven. Should this happen it is possible either to damage or shorten the life of the magnetron. Thus, it is very important to adhere to the manufacturer's instructions regarding operation.

Interior oven light Many ovens are supplied with interior oven lights which can prove useful if the oven is accommodated in a poorly lit area. In some instances where the oven has a 'clear' door this feature enables the user to observe the food being cooked without the necessity of opening the door. However, this particular benefit is very much dependent upon the lighting conditions of the room, as if the light intensity within the room is high then the oven interior light will not necessarily give sufficient illumination for the outside observation of food.

Splatter shields and guards In some instances the wave stirrer (paddle) is protected from any splashes that may occur by a protective shield. This is generally removable and should be kept clean in accordance with the manufacturer's instructions.

Oven shelf A removable glass or plastics shelf may be housed on the base of the oven floor and as it is an integral part of the oven design it should always be used as recommended. However, as it is of a special quality it should never be replaced with any other form of glass or plastics if accidently broken. The purpose of the shelf can be to act as a spillage plate, to protect the magnetron should the oven be accidently operated without a food load, or to ensure that the food and containers are situated in the best position in the oven. Generally, it is suspended an inch or so from the oven floor and the food to be heated or cooked is placed in a container on this shelf. Thus, as the microwaves strike the oven floor they then pass through the shelf, ensuring that the food is given the utmost benefit of the microwaves. Nevertheless, if a shelf is not supplied it must be remembered that the manufacturer may have considered it not necessary for his particular oven design.

Built-in browning element A built-in browning element is not a common feature on microwave ovens but when fitted its purpose is to enable the user to brown foods by the use of a conventional element housed at the top of the microwave oven, thus avoiding the necessity of employing another conventional appliance in the kitchen for browning purposes.

Browning plates, dishes and skillets As a basic microwave oven is not capable of browning foods some manufacturers supply, as an optional extra, a special dish designed primarily for browning foods in the microwave oven. This dish is only intended for use in the microwave oven and is not suitable for use in or on conventional top heating surfaces.

By using a browning dish the range of cooking can be increased to include such items as pancakes, 'fried' eggs, toasted sandwiches, etc. In addition to which the use of the browning dish gives added eye appeal to food items such as steaks, chops and the like. The shape of the dish can vary depending upon the manufacturer, but in general it is made of a glass ceramic material supported on small feet and has a special coating on the bottom which is heated by the microwaves to a higher temperature than the food would normally be. The empty browning dish is pre-heated for different times depending upon the food to be cooked. Once pre-heated, the food is placed on the dish and the surface of the food is then seared and browned. During the cooking period the food is reversed to obtain browning on the reverse side. Unlike most dishes used in the oven some browning dishes can get very, very hot, and therefore they should be handled with care, and if they are placed on a work surface during or after use it is advisable to place a protective tray underneath.

However, some manufacturers supply a detachable handle for the dish which adds to easier handling. When cleaning the dish, care should be exercised not to damage the coating, but if a scouring pad is necessary, then only a plastics type should be used and this may only be applied on the topside of the dish. Nevertheless, it is important to observe any specific instruction given by the manufacturer.

A browning dish and skillet

Cooking container kits Some manufacturers can supply, as an optional extra, complete cooking container kits which have been specially designed and made for the microwave oven user. Thus, the kit would cover those shapes and sizes of containers which are likely to be of most benefit in the home, whilst being of the best shape for the food being cooked. The range is extensive and includes such items as measuring jugs to casseroles, bowls, pie dishes, bread dishes, ramekin dishes etc. In some cases it is also possible to obtain a special roasting dish complete with trivet which may be used to support the meat or poultry on the trivet whilst retaining the juices in the container.

Cooking container kit

Meat and food thermometers At no time should meat or food thermometers be used in the microwave oven unless the manufacturer specifically states that this is possible, but even in these instances the method of use is important and any manufacturer's instructions should be strictly observed. Some manufacturers can supply a thermometer (as an optional extra) which has been specially designed for their particular oven. The thermometer, in general, will have a pointed probe which is inserted into the meat or food and for convenience a dial giving the various degrees of temperature is fixed at the top of the probe. As the temperature of the food increases a pointer moves up the scale indicating the temperature within the food. As would be expected, it is not possible to view the dial of the thermometer through a door and it would therefore be necessary for a user to periodically open the door and check the reading.

Revolving platforms During the normal cooking or heating process of food in a microwave oven it is necessary, on occasions, to either stir the food or turn the dish within the oven to obtain even heating of the food. One manufacturer produces an oven which incorporates a revolving platform. The foodstuffs are placed in the container on the revolving platform and this automatically turns throughout the heating and cooking process.

Sharp Electronics microwave oven showing revolving platform

Portable trolleys Although a microwave oven can be moved around it may prove inconvenient to physically carry it from room to room. In which case, a sturdy trolley on wheels can be obtained as an optional extra and this would accommodate the microwave oven on the top shelf, whilst the lower shelf or shelves could be used for other purposes.

Instruction and recipe books It is a known fact that the average user of any product rarely refers to an instruction book until something inconvenient occurs. However, as microwave ovens are rather new it is more than likely that a new user will welcome some form of instruction and recipe book.

Invariably a new oven is always supplied with both, and it is obvious from the style and presentation of these books that a great deal of thought and effort has been put into the final publication. As with anything new it is a great temptation to either scan or disregard any reading matter and enjoy the benefits of the new purchase. With a microwave oven more use and fun can be obtained if the manufacturer's books are read first. Apart

A Thermador microwave oven complete with trolley

from the obvious reasons for reading the book first, the microwave oven is so versatile that many new and exciting cooking methods can be employed which perhaps the new user had not thought possible.

It is not usual to examine the instruction and recipe book of an appliance before purchase but in the case of microwave ovens they are worthy of perusal at the onset, as the book itself will be the first and main influence on the type of use the user will give the microwave oven. A point which is to be considered when examining any book is to check if the recipes relate to the type of

66

foods which are generally available to the user, and that the recipes are of the right type. Nevertheless, once the choice has been made it is important to follow the manufacturer's instructions as this will not only give the user plenty of well tried advice but also open up a new world of cooking and food preparation.

A brief look to the future At present in the USA and Canada, it is not unusual to see a microwave oven unit as part of the kitchen scene being used as an appliance and not just as part of the fittings. In Europe, although used quite extensively in the catering industry, the microwave oven is on the brink of 'discovery' as more and more members of the general public become aware of its use and advantages. Nevertheless, if the initial purchase price is beyond the average pocket the benefits can only be enjoyed by a few. However, over the past five years, as the demand for microwave ovens has increased so the price has decreased and as a result many more people are able to appreciate this 'new' appliance. Indeed, it has been said that the home ownership of microwave ovens in Great Britain could be in the region of 10,000—25,000 by 1978. This figure would seem quite feasible if the trend of the USA is examined where microwave ovens have been generally available for longer than in Europe. In 1970, 80,000 domestic microwave ovens were sold but by 1976 this had increased to 1·66 million. (Source: R. E. A. Bott—Amana Refrigeration Inc.)

The basic microwave oven will continue to be of benefit both today and tomorrow but as is to be expected changes will be made to keep abreast with the needs or demands of the user. It could be tempting to discuss future developments in such a way as to be almost unrealistic even though almost anything is possible. However, it is more interesting to discuss a future which is within reach.

In both the USA and Germany microwave ovens are just beginning to be part of the domestic cooker. These cookers have the external appearance of a conventional appliance with either a ceramic hob or conventional hotplates.

However, the oven itself combines the efficiency of microwave with the benefits of conventional heat. Added to which the user has a choice of being able to use either microwave or conventional heating for cooking, or both together. Nevertheless, even with this benefit a further choice is possible as the oven may be of the forced air type (fan assisted) or of the conventionally heated type but with a self clean facility.

Beekay Bauknecht cooker model MH800

As some users may prefer to keep the conventional and the new separate, a double oven cooker has been designed which gives the user the benefit of a conventionally heated main oven but a microwave second oven.

Controls are likely to change and be improved, adding to the ease of use. For example, the facia would show a list of operations such as baking, roasting, casserole cooking, etc., and all the operator will be required to do is to press the adjacent button. Touch controls, which are just beginning to be available on conventional appliances could perhaps become a standard type of control on microwave ovens. Indeed, there is at least one microwave oven in the USA with touch controls which does away with the need to turn dials or push buttons.

In addition, the use of digital clocks is likely to be introduced thus contributing to a quicker and easier method of selecting and observing the times set for an operation.

As can be appreciated the scope and design for microwave ovens is exciting and interesting, and it is almost impossible to envisage what the future will hold. It is an appliance of today's world giving the user more versatility and convenience in both living and cooking; yet, it is an appliance which will not rest on its laurels but change and advance to suit the needs of future generations.

Freezing hot cover and mat An exclusive feature of one manufacturer is a mat and cover which is designed to reduce the likelihood of dehydration around the edges of frozen products during the thawing process.

The accessory comprises a round ceramic mat complete with a metal cover, similar to that of a plate cover. As the cover has a plastics handle, and the underside also accommodates a ceramic disc enclosed in plastics, the microwaves are only able to pass through these areas. The ceramic is of a type which retains heat and therefore contributes to the thawing process.

To use the accessory the frozen food is placed in its container on the ceramic mat, covered with the metal cover and the oven is then operated in the usual manner.

Special hot cover and mat. *Merrychef Ltd*

CHAPTER 7
Cooking utensils and containers

Before embarking on this chapter it should be noted that the word 'container' includes any form of material or shape which will either contain or support foods, e.g. cups, plates, bowls, jugs, etc.

It is common practice to have countless utensils and containers in the kitchen for the preparation and sometimes for the serving of food. In addition to which, table china and glass is, in general, used exclusively for table service and is unlikely to be used for any other purpose. Indeed, the various categories of containers are usually limited by the type of heat, if any, that can be applied and care in use is important. However, as a microwave oven will accommodate almost every conceivable material and shape with the exception of metal and some plastics, a new world of convenience is available to the user. So far as containers are

Food containers supplied by *Corning Housecraft Service*

concerned the advantages of using them in the microwave oven extend beyond versatility.

1) The container will remain relatively cool to handle—any heat will be as a result of the hot food transferring its heat to the container.

2) The hazard of handling extremely hot containers is reduced.

3) Frozen food from the freezer can be placed directly into the microwave oven for thawing, heating and/or cooking.

4) Food can be cooked in containers to be served directly to the table.

5) Individual portions or whole dishes can be reheated in minutes for microwave-to-table service.

6) Fewer utensils and containers will be used, thus less washing up.

As existing containers, utensils and table ware are more versatile, less storage space will be required.

The best container to use is one which is non-porous, allows the microwaves to be transmitted into the food and will not melt or warp. Any container which reflects the microwaves away from the food, absorbs microwaves or melts due to the heat or steam from the food is unsuitable. A further point to remember is that should the oven have a browning element or if auxiliary radiant heating such as a grill is to be used then the material must not be flammable.

The shape and size of the utensil is important, and it is worthwhile following the guide given by almost all microwave oven manufacturers in their respective cookery books.

Round or regular shapes are better as those having acute corners allow more exposure to the microwaves, and as a result the food in these corner areas would tend to 'dry out'. Oval shapes, although not having acute corners, can in certain cooking operations show the same tendencies at the narrower ends of the container. Almost any size of container may be used but due to the unique application of microwaves for heating and cooking a more even, and faster result is achieved if the best size is selected. For example, vegetables would cook more quickly if they were cooked in a container which would allow them to be spread out as an even layer rather than lumping them in a narrow high sided container which would increase the overall depth of the vegetables. However, in other instances it would be unwise to use a shallow container. For example, as milk and milk based dishes have a tendency to boil, the choice of a deeper container would avoid the inconvenience of boiling over.

When thawing foods the size should be large enough to accommodate the thawed mass yet of the right shape to give the best cooking result. However, should a block of frozen food require thawing then the container should be of such a shape that as the ice melts the liquid will not be able to spread over a wide area. (See Chapter 2 *Thawing foods*.)

In general it is better to select a container which allows the food to be of the same depth, thus ensuring that it all gets the same benefit from the microwaves, but should a larger quantity of food be heated or cooked then the centre of the area should have less depth of food than the outer. Nevertheless, this may be used to advantage if foods requiring more cooking are accommodated around the outer areas. Although this principle applies in general it must be remembered that as dish rotation, stirring and turning over food is part of the procedure this, too, should be taken into consideration. (See Chapter 2 *The art of thawing, heating and cooking*.)

Utensil and container materials

It is difficult to cover every type of utensil or container likely to be available in the home and only guidance can be given. However, a simple test can be conducted to ascertain the suitability of the utensil for use in the oven. This is carried out by placing a cup filled with water in or on the container being tested. These are put into the oven and the timer is set for $1\frac{1}{4}$ minutes. After which time the water, cup, and container are removed. If the water is warm and the container cool, it is suitable for use. However, if the container is slightly warm around the edges and the water is luke warm then it is only suitable for short periods of heating food. Conversely, if the container is very warm or hot and the water cool it is not advisable to use it in the oven. What has happened is that the container is absorbing the microwaves and as a result will not give the food the full benefit of all the microwave energy available. Where a test is needed for table glass or plastics the same procedure is carried out but the timer is only set for ten to fifteen seconds to ensure that should the container heat up it will not be damaged unnecessarily. Should the glass or plastics feel warm then it is unsuitable for use in the oven.

The following list is given as a guide and may be used to establish principles. However, it is always advisable to read the microwave oven manufacturer's instruction book, but if there is any doubt as to the suitability of any particular container, the supplier of either the oven or container should be consulted. Particular care should be taken when reading the instruction book as if it has been compiled abroad the definition of a material may be different to that found in the country of use.

Straw and wood are materials which would not normally be used for cooking but may be used in a microwave oven for short heating operations such as warming bread rolls in a basket just before serving. However, wooden utensils or containers used in the oven for prolonged periods of time do have a tendency to dry out.

Paper is available in many forms and can be found in the shape of plates, cups, towels and serviettes. The use of this material will not only be useful but also convenient, as it can cut down the unnecessary chore of washing up plates and such like. Paper towels are invaluable when the moisture from foods needs to be absorbed, an example of this being bread products which when heated tend to give off moisture and if the moisture is not absorbed the product can prove to be soggy.

Greaseproof paper is a simple material to use when a covering lid is needed or as a means of preventing food spattering the oven.

Waxed paper plates, cups and dishes are not particularly successful as the high temperature reached by the food is likely to cause the wax coating to melt; therefore, if this form of material is used it should be with care and only for very short operations.

Cotton or linen napkins or towels may be preferred or be more convenient to use and there is no reason why this material should not be used for short periods. However, the fabric must be 100% cotton or linen and not contain any synthetic fibres.

Table glass in the form of wine glasses, tumblers, grapefruit dishes and other similar containers, may be used in the oven for short operations but it is important to note that antique or fragile glass could break if the food it contains is going to reach such a high temperature that the heat from the food is likely to be transferred to the glass. Nevertheless, the benefit of using glass can be endless; baked grapefruit, hot toddies, and hot fruit salad can all be prepared and heated in the dish ready for service to the table.

Oven to table glass, and glass ceramic containers are likely to be suitable but as the ingredients of them vary it is advisable to test the container to establish its suitability before using it. In many instances, this type of utensil is also suitable for the freezer and its versatility can then be extended to take in food preparation, freezing, thawing, and heating in the microwave oven and then serving to the table. If, however, any glassware contains or is decorated with metal it is not for use in a microwave oven.

China in the form of earthenware, pottery, stoneware, porcelain and bone china are on the whole acceptable providing that they are free of metal (as with glassware) but as there can be such a variety in the home it is advisable to check test it first. It is also advisable not to use cups and the like where the handles have been glued on as the glue can melt and make the handle insecure.

Plastics The best type of plastics for use in a microwave oven are thermoplastics which can tolerate very high temperatures of 150°–200°C (300°–400°F). Plastics are available in many guises and can be readily obtained for cups, saucers, bowls, plates and almost any other form required. Although the microwave oven will accommodate plastics it should always be check tested first. If the container is deemed suitable it is wise to use it for heating up foods rather than for cooking them, as prolonged cooking raises the temperature of the food to such a degree that this can cause the plastics to distort, melt or shrivel. A further point to remember is that if foods have a high fat or sugar content then the use of plastics should be avoided.

Plastics cling type film is a convenient aid to the microwave oven user especially as a lining for containers, or for wrapping foods. However, if it is employed to form a tight covering lid or wrapping then a small slit should be made to allow steam from the food to escape.

Boil in the bag pouches can be used with confidence and are of particular use to the freezer owner. The complete bag can be placed in the oven and the thawing or short heating period may be carried out very quickly. As with plastics film it is necessary to make a small slit in the bag to ensure an escape of steam.

Roasting bags are of benefit especially as a method of browning joints of meat. However, the metal ties must be replaced by string and the bag should be pricked to allow for the escape of steam.

Plastics storage type bags should never be used as the heat from the food will cause them to melt. The only exception to this statement would occur where the plastics is of the type which could tolerate the high temperature attained by the food.

Metal in general is simple to identify and *must not be used* in a microwave oven and it should be remembered that some utensils and containers do include metal in the container ingredients, thus these too, are unsuitable. Furthermore, if any container has any form of metal decoration, i.e. gold leaf, 'arcing' within the oven would occur and this would shorten its life or damage the magnetron. Remember that metal reflects microwaves away from the food so why waste time and effort?

Foil Some ovens are designed to allow the use of a limited amount of foil and this in certain instances can be beneficial, but foil should never be employed unless it is recommended by the manufacturer and then it should only be used in accordance with the manufacturer's instructions. In addition to which, if foil is used it must not be allowed to touch any part of the oven interior.

General information

Although containers will remain relatively cool during use (as the ideal one will not absorb the microwaves), they could get hot if the food within attains very high temperatures and in these instances some heat would transfer to the container itself. However, the container temperatures are less likely to reach those usually found in conventional cooking.

Covers and wrapping food is not always needed; however if

covers are required the choice of material is wide and it will not be necessary to use only those containers with matching lids. (See Chapter 2 *Covering and wrapping foods.*)

Should a cover be employed it should not be used so tightly that steam is unable to escape.

When selecting a container for use in a thawing, heating or cooking operation three points should be remembered: 1) use a container made of the right material; 2) select a container to suit the size and shape of the food; and 3) in the case of liquids, one large enough to prevent the contents from boiling over.

CHAPTER 8
Cleaning the appliance

Cleaning a microwave oven bears no relation to the chore that most have experienced with a conventional oven. The main reason for this is because all the energy is concentrated into the food and the oven interior remains relatively cool. So if by chance any splashing has occurred it does not 'burn on' any hot surface. However, should a spillage of food occur during the time the oven is in use it would be wise to wipe it up immediately—microwaves cannot differentiate between food to be cooked in a container and food which has been spilled, so don't waste the microwave energy!

Under no circumstances should the oven be dismantled without specific instructions from the microwave oven manufacturer and just like a conventional cooker it would be advisable to disconnect the appliance from the supply before carrying out a major cleaning operation.

After the appliance has been used the oven interior and door should be wiped over with a damp cloth and unless specifically recommended by a manufacturer proprietary cleaners in any form must never be used. There may, however, be an occasion when a small amount of soil proves to be stubborn to remove but the temptation to attack it with a scouring pad or a proprietary cleaning agent must be resisted. Should this condition occur, a quantity of water in a non-metallic container could be heated in the oven and the vapour would then help to loosen the soil which would be easily removed with a damp cloth.

Some ovens have a splatter guard over the stirrer (paddle) in the top of the oven interior and/or an air filter. Both of these should be checked frequently and removed for cleaning in accordance with the manufacturer's instructions. However, in general it would simply be a case of washing them in warm soapy water, rinsing, and after drying with a soft cloth fitting them back into the oven. Should an oven be fitted with a removable base, glass or plastics shelf it is cleaned as the splatter guard or air filter would be, but should it be broken by accident then it must only be replaced by the manufacturer and no other type of glass or plastics should be used.

As in conventional cooking some strong flavoured foods may result in the oven having an odour, but if this happens the odour can be removed by boiling some water and lemon juice in a container in the oven for a minute or two.

If the exterior requires cleaning a wipe over with a damp cloth would be sufficient but care should be exercised to ensure that no water is splashed over the exterior vents.

A word of caution. It is important that the door seal is perfect, therefore care should be taken that this area is kept clean and free of soil and at no time should a sharp implement such as a knife be used to dislodge soil, and under no circumstances should abrasives or proprietary cleaners be used to clean either the door or seal. Should any damage occur in this area the oven must not be used until it has been checked by a service engineer.

CHAPTER 9
Capital, maintenance and running costs

The question of capital, running and maintenance costs would on the surface appear to be a relatively simple problem. However, because the microwave oven is such a unique and versatile appliance the issue becomes rather more complex. Bold words can be used but all are supported by side benefits which, when examined, can undermine a straight forward comparison with other appliances. In addition to which, just as the advantages of a microwave oven are determined by the user so are the cost benefits whether these be in the form of money, time, convenience or comfort. Nevertheless, an attempt may be made to examine the costs related to microwave ovens and at the same time the side benefits should also be taken into consideration as these contribute to an overall appreciation of the concept of microwave.

Installation

Most homes today will already have a suitably earthed socket outlet in the kitchen and as a result the cost of installing a microwave oven is in general, simply the price of a plug.

The purchase price

The actual price of a microwave oven will very much depend upon the oven selected-and the features available. However, at the time of writing domestic models are available for about £200–£400, and catering models enter a higher price group as the size, outputs and features are intended for a different market and these are about £400–£1000. Moving above this in the catering area and examining the Mealstream system, which represents a cooker, the purchase price would be in the region of £2400. In view of the choice available it would be difficult to state a specific figure. Nevertheless, if an average domestic unit is considered then the cost can compare more than favourably with such leisure goods as coloured televisions and stereo units which, in many of today's homes, are considered to be part of the furniture. Indeed, it is interesting to note that both a television and a stereo unit are regarded as a means of entertainment and it is accepted that both have their own specific way of giving it.

A similar analogy could be made with a microwave oven and a conventional cooker: both can have a place in the kitchen but each will have something to contribute. However, in this instance, and unlike the television and stereo unit, they may be used to complement each other thus giving the user a wider and more convenient method of operation.

Maintenance

The first question which is likely to be asked is, what could go wrong? However, although the microwave oven appears to be more remarkable than many other appliances, in many ways it is less complicated. Therefore, providing that it is used correctly and not abused there should be no reason why it should not give years of trouble free service. Needless to say the heart of the oven is the magnetron which is likely to give something like four to six thousand hours of use but like most appliances this figure could well be exceeded. Indeed, the guarantee period could be up to five years which would indicate the confidence the manufacturers have in this part. However, when the time comes, the cost of replacing the magnetron can be quite high but just like a television it is sometimes possible to enter into a service contract with some manufacturers. So far as home service calls are concerned, each manufacturer will have a very efficient back up service but it would be advisable for a prospective purchaser to discuss this factor at the time of comparing ovens.

Running costs

The running costs of the microwave oven can be very low bearing in mind that all the microwave energy is concentrated into the product being thawed, heated or cooked. Consequently, the need to preheat an oven is not required and there is very little, if any, loss of heat as would be experienced with conventional appliances. Therefore, on this basis alone the running costs could be expected to be less if a comparison was to be made between the two.

A study made by Amana Refrigeration Inc. demonstrated

energy savings by cooking 55 out of 77 items with a median saving of 63%. It would be misleading to say that the microwave oven will always prove to be an energy saving appliance as much would depend on the quantities of food being cooked and the type of operation being employed. Indeed, as has been previously discussed the initial temperature, the structure of the food, the container accommodating the food, the output of the oven, and the actual cooking time given by the user will all have an influence on the final energy figure. Nevertheless, the running cost of the microwave oven can contribute to the conservation of energy but as Tables 5 and 6 indicate the actual amount will be dependent upon the individual's cooking requirements. In addition, although in general the use of a microwave oven will reduce energy consumption it should be noted that the oven could be employed to carry out such operations as the thawing or reheating of food. In which case energy will be used where previously food may have been thawed at room temperature or eaten in the cold state. It should be remembered that the other side benefits of a microwave oven may compensate; these include the saving of time and the added convenience and the saving of energy in other directions.

Table 5. Energy consumption in microwave cooking compared to conventional cooking

Fresh Product	Method of Cooking	kWh
4 Chicken pieces	Microwave Conventional oven	0·402 1·139
Topside of beef	Microwave Conventional oven	0·411 1·723
Wholemeal bread	Microwave Conventional oven	0·097 0·914
Apple suet pudding	Microwave Hotplate	0·226 0·633
Pineapple upside down cake	Microwave Conventional hotplate/oven	0·147 1·018
2 Herrings	Microwave Grill	0·037 0·213

Source: Electricity Council Appliance Testing Laboratories

Table 6. Energy consumption in microwave cooking compared to conventional cooking: vegetables

Fresh Product	Method of Cooking	kWh
Brussel Sprouts	Microwave	0·10
	Hotplate	0·20
Mushrooms	Microwave	0·08
	Hotplate	0·18
Boiled potatoes	Microwave	0·28
	Hotplate	0·26
Boiled parsnips	Microwave	0·27
	Hotplate	0·30
White cabbage	Microwave	0·24
	Hotplate	0·24
Leeks	Microwave	0·27
	Hotplate	0·24
Sweet peppers	Microwave	0·09
	Hotplate	0·26
Cauliflower flourets	Microwave	0·27
	Hotplate	0·20

Source: Electricity Council Appliance Testing Laboratories

The side benefits

Time The value of saving time can only be measured by the individual and it is only he or she who can put a figure on it. The microwave oven can save time in so much that it may be used as an 'instant' appliance thus producing thawed, heated, reheated or cooked foods in a fraction of the time it would take if conventional methods were employed. Self imposed banishment to the kitchen may be disregarded and as extra time is available, the user may extend the day to include other interests or work. On the other hand for those who regard cooking as a hobby and pleasure more time is available to prepare and make new or more dishes.

Convenience Like time, convenience of using a microwave oven will depend upon the individual, as what is convenient to one may not be for another. Nevertheless, convenience could be considered to be one or more of the following:

82

□ A quick method of thawing foods when they are required rather than having to think about thawing them hours prior to eating.

□ A clean and simple way in which to reheat plated or individual foods.

□ Reducing the need to pre-think menus.

□ Being able to heat or cook food when the desire to eat occurs.

□ Less chores to do such as washing up—even heating a hot dog can be done using a paper napkin.

□ Almost anyone of any age can manipulate the oven.

□ The microwave oven can be situated and moved with relative ease from room to room.

□ Cleaning the appliance is minimal.

□ Special foods or diets can be catered for.

Comfort As all the energy is concentrated at once into the food being cooked, preheating the oven is not necessary—added to which the food cooks more quickly, and this in itself means that the oven is relatively cool. Consequently the loss of heat from the oven is negligible and the kitchen becomes a cooler place in which to work. Apart from the physical comfort, for those who have air conditioning in their homes, because the microwave oven is so cool the conditioning does not have to contend with any extra heat and consequently can cost less to operate.

Labour It is unlikely that the home user will feel that the question of labour is an important aspect mainly because labour in the home does not have a price put on it. However, in the catering environment this can be an important factor especially as labour costs are so high. The microwave oven can help the caterer to give an even better service with the minimum of labour and whether this be skilled or unskilled would in no way detract from the service to the customer.

Floor space Convenience in siting the oven is important to both the home user and the caterer, but the caterer is very aware that every square metre of floor space has to be paid for and is part of the overall running costs of the establishment. Thus, this must in some way be passed on to the customer. However, as the microwave oven does not necessarily have to take up floor space, any area gained may be employed for other purposes which may add to an efficient and more economical use of space in the kitchen, bar, restaurant, etc.

Kitchen decorations As the microwave oven is such a clean appliance to use, the need to re-decorate is less likely to arise and as a result the kitchen maintenance costs could be reduced.

A question of conservation

Conservation is a word which is on the lips of everyone in today's world and can be associated with the past, present and future but in every instance the present will relate to both the past and the future. Traditions, the environment, foods and raw materials are amongst many which can be discussed. Certainly in the 1970's a number of countries have learnt, by necessity, to be aware of the wise use of so much which before has been taken for granted. It has been said that 'every little counts' and this has been demonstrated many times. However, to illustrate the point: a dripping tap can waste in 30 minutes, something like a litre of water ($1\frac{3}{4}$ pints). In twenty four hours this is in the region of 48 litres (84 pints). Multiply this figure by only ten houses in a town and the waste of water becomes a remarkable figure of 480 litres (105 gallons). Thus, to discuss conservation in relation to the microwave oven is not quite as dramatic as would first appear.

The question of the energy required has been discussed so it is unnecessary to expand on this subject. However, because less cooking utensils will need to be used and 'oven to table' ware can be used more frequently less washing up is required. The result, less energy to heat water, and less detergent and water will be used. A small benefit standing alone but, like a dripping tap when multiplied, it can show an interesting figure.

The quantity of water used to cook vegetables by conventional means is, in general, far more than is necessary, yet when using a microwave oven the amount will be minimal or none at all. (See *Table 2.*)

The wastage of food can be reduced as the actual amount required can be heated or cooked as and when desired. Cold food and drinks are less likely to be thrown out but reheated—how many cups of coffee have been discarded because they had been left to get cold? Home freezer owners can select dishes only a short time before they are needed thus the chance of being

84

obliged to use food just because it had thawed out all day is less likely. However, as always, each user will soon get used to the idea and as a result wastage will be a thing of the past as they find their own ways of making wise use of the oven and less waste of the food.

At the beginning of this chapter it was said that the capital, maintenance and running costs was not a simple project and certainly the more the subject is examined it confirms, that like life, there is more to it than meets the eye. Nevertheless, the overall costs of using a microwave oven are more than likely to err on the plus side but as to the percentage of the plus, this will be influenced by the user and will also depend upon what he or she considers to be the plus factor.

Talking about conventional cookers

The basic microwave oven is such that as mentioned previously, it should not really be compared to the conventional cooker but many will do so even though there is a place for both in the home. In view of this, it is worth taking a brief look at the two to enable considered opinions to be formed as to why the conventional cooker should not be compared.

Both the microwave oven and the conventional cooker can carry out similar operations but in some instances the two will not necessarily be able to complete the same sort of job; on the other hand one or the other will be the better appliance for a specific operation. Disregarding the many benefits of the microwave and examining perhaps the basic differences, the conventional cooker can accommodate much larger quantities and a greater variety of food at the same time but the whole operation will take some time to complete. However, because of its size and its method of applying heat it can prove to be an uneconomical appliance to use where smaller quantities of food are to be heated or cooked.

At the time of writing a basic gas or electic cooker could cost in the region of £150. This of course does not include any installation costs which could apply in the case of any piping or electrical wiring.

Maintenance costs will have to be considered although most cookers carry at least a one year guarantee. So far as maintenance is concerned, it would be difficult to assess what, if anything, would be required. However, over the time a cooker is in use, it may continue to be operative and as a result the user will 'put up with' any fault rather than arrange for a service call. Finally, the user will make a decision to either have the cooker serviced and get the various faults rectified or take the opportunity to buy a new appliance.

It can only be repeated that the basic microwave oven, at the moment, is not intended to replace the conventional family cooker but is intended to aid the user and to add a more convenient and in many instances, a more economical method of food preparation in the home.

Indeed, it may be worth remembering that already other appliances are used for various purposes where the specific operation could be carried out on the conventional cooker. Looking around a kitchen it is more than likely that one or more of the following can be found: coffee makers, infra-red contact grills, heated trays and trolleys, kettles, electric frypans, roasting spits, milk warmers, and so on. It is therefore likely that, in the future, the user may prefer to glean the benefits of both the conventional cooker and the basic microwave oven by choosing a less expensive standard cooker to use alongside a basic microwave oven. However, for those who already have a conventional cooker then the microwave oven may be considered to be another asset in the home adding to the richness of life.

Glossary of terms

Electrical terms

Ampere	The unit of current flow.
Anode	The electron collector in a thermionic valve.
Arc	An electrical discharge maintained in ionised air or gas.
Capacitor	A component formed by thin metal plates separated by a dielectric which may be vacuum, waxed or oiled paper, glass, plastic, foil, etc.
Cathode	The electron emitter of a thermionic valve.
Electro-magnetic wave	A wave formed of time—dependent mutually—perpendicular electric and magnetic fields. The spectrum of electro-magnetic waves includes radio waves, heat and light rays, ultra-violet rays, X-rays, and gamma rays.
High voltage	A voltage above 650 volts.
Ionizing radiation	Any electro-magnetic or particulate radiation which produces ion pairs when passing through a medium.
Magnetron	A thermionic tube containing an anode and a heated cathode, the flow of electrons from cathode to anode being controlled by an externally applied magnetic field and designed for generating microwave energy.
mW/cm^2	Milliwatts per square centimetre; the unit used for the measurement of radiated power.
Power transformer	Transformer providing high tension and filament (low tension) supplies in electronic equipment.
Rectifier	A component for converting a.c. into d.c. by inversion or suppression of alternate half waves.
Watt	The unit of power corresponding to the rate of expenditure of energy.
Waveguide	Hollow metal conductor within which microwave energy can be transmitted efficiently.
Volt	The unit of electrical pressure or electromotive force.

General terms

B.S.	British Standard
cm	Centimetre
ins	Inches
mm	Millimetre
ml	Millilitre
Molecule	The smallest part of an element or compound which exhibits all the chemical properties of that specific compound or element.
lb.	Pound (weight)
oz.	Ounce
gr.	Gram
Kg	Kilogram

Bibliography

An Exciting new World of Microwave Cooking
by Litton Microwave Cooking Products Ltd. Pillsbury Publications, USA.

A Guide to Microwave Catering by Lewis Napleton.
Northwood Industrial Publications Ltd.

A Guide to Systemized Catering by Lewis Napleton.
Northwood Industrial Publications Ltd.

Cooking with Microwaves. Volume 6
International Microwave Power Institute. (IMPI), Canada.

Marvels of Microwave by Corning Glass Works, USA.

Microwave Heating of Food—changes in nutrient and chemical composition by Klaus Lorenz. CRC Press, USA.

Instructors' Teaching Guide by Amana Refrigeration Inc., Iowa, USA.

Mealstream Cooking Guide by Mealstream Catering Systems.

Acknowledgements

Apollo Enterprises

Beekay Bauknecht

Birds Eye Foods Ltd.

R. E. A. Bott (Wigmore Street) Ltd.

British Airways

British Celanese Ltd.

British Food Manufacturing Industries Research Association

British Rail

Corning Housecraft Service

Electricity Council Marketing Department, Appliance Testing Laboratories, and Catering Centre

Hirst Electric Industri,s (Mealstream)

Litton Microwave Cooking Products Ltd.

Long Aston Research Station

Loughborough University of Technology

Merrychef Ltd.

National Panasonic (UK) Ltd.

Philips Electrical Ltd.

Queen Elizabeth College, University of London

Sharp Electronics (UK) Ltd.

Tappan International Ltd.

Thorn Domestic Appliances (Electrical) Ltd.

Toshiba (UK) Limited, Microwave Oven Division